BEHIND THE FENCE

PAUL GOSS

Index

Dedicated to my long suffering wife Kaz

And my mum Bren. x

Behind the Fence

I have seen and heard things you would not believe. You may well read the true stories in this book and think that they are the creation of a strange and twisted individual, pure fiction from the mind of a fool. Well that's fine. I am a bit strange, and I am a bit twisted. Since starting this job, I have had experiences that would upset the toughest stomach, scare the hardest man and penetrate the thickest of skins. There have been serious assaults and attacks. I have seen death on a number of occasions. I've witnessed illness, strange perversions, outrageous human behaviour that you would witness nowhere else in the world, other than any other prison.

I have lost count of the amount of times I've heard these words said, "Someone should write a book about that". I have said it myself. I have been waiting years for someone to step forward and start writing. There are loads of amusing anecdotes, funny observations and hilarious stories of the things that happen inside the walls. There have also been hundreds of nasty incidents including serious assaults, self harm, attempted murder and mutilation. All officers in the service have their favourite story. We see the most amazing behaviour day after day, year after year, the strange goings on behind the fence. It is now time to be that person. I must be the one to step forward and share the wonderful happenings with you, the disbelieving public.

The one thing that prison staff, have in common is their ability to see the funny side. I have contacted many friends in the writing of this book. I have drawn on vast experience within the service to put this book together. Officers with forty years experience, down to officers who have only just started on the long and arduous road that is a prison career, have all made their contributions. I aim to present the cream of the stories to you in this, my first book. I want you to experience the best of the bunch, the ones that we as officers continue to recall years after they have happened. In those boring moments on the landings or in the office, when the clock seems to be going backwards, these are the tales that help to get us through the day.

Obviously all the poor unfortunates who are having their stories recalled and recounted here need some sort of protection. I have decided to change all the prisoner's names to "Smith". I don't want to be rude or disrespectful to anyone with the name Smith but there does seem to be a lot of them in Prison. I think this is a numbers game rather than unusually bad behaviour by the Smith's. So this name will be used to protect the innocent, or in most of these cases the guilty!

Also, I feel it necessary, as I can't remember the original names of some the people featured in this book, to apologise to anyone who are or were, actually called Smith. You're cover has now been blown, and your story told to millions. Well, probably more like tens, but what the hell?

At the same time I think the staff mentioned also need a bit of protection. If I mention anyone I know and then they read this, I may be putting myself in grave danger.

Some of these guys are bloody big lads you know. So indirectly, the name changes are for my protection. For no reason other than the fact this is a common surname, the main officer in each story will be called Jones. I don't think any of the actual staff involved were called Jones but just in case, sorry once again.

In order to fully understand my reasons for writing this book I feel I should let you know the basics of how a prison works. There will obviously be variations from prison to prison so I will describe an average, across the board sort of day.

Staff arrive by about 07:30 and carry out roll checks. This is important, as we need to make sure that nobody has decided to leave us in the night. Obviously this would cause major problems with the usual regime and the list of things that follow would be curtailed. In the unusual event of an escape, looking for missing prisoner duties would take over.

At about 08:00 the prisoners are unlocked and have their breakfast. This comes in various forms. Anything from cereal to toast or porridge to full cooked English could be on the menu depending on what day it is. The food is served from a Servery. The Servery is sometimes on the wing and caters for the prisoners on that wing. Sometimes there is a central Servery that caters for all the wings at once. The prisoners file through with their plates and bowls to collect whatever is on offer. The latest trend though, is to dish out "Breakfast Packs" with the dinner meal so that the con's can eat their breakfast in the morning without the need to visit the Servery at all. The Pack contains a very small amount of cereal, a tea bag, a sugar sachet, some milk powder and a carton of long life milk. Not really enough to feed a small child, but it is the Home Offices' latest great money saving idea. The fact that most of the cons take the pack and then throw the bits they don't want in the bin or out of the window is immaterial. The Home Office says it saves money, so it does!

 On the subject of throwing things out of the window, this is something I have never worked out. Prisoners throw stuff out of their windows! I don't know why? They all have bins in their cells. There are bigger bins on the landings to empty their small bins into. Yet it is necessary in every prison to employ an "Outside Cleaner" whose job it is to go round and pick up all the crap that the cons have thrown out. Talking of crap, in a lot of places, (especially the ones without toilets in the cells), they even throw out their poo. These are known as shit parcels and come in many forms. Ranging from poo in a T-shirt, poo in a bag, poo wrapped in toilet roll. That's quite posh, as they don't usually like to waste their toilet roll in that way. But the piece de resistance is the newspaper wrapped poo. This looks rather like the bundle you collect from the Chippie when you buy your supper but with much more sinister innards. WHY?? Why would anyone do that? Most prisoners now have 24-hour access to a toilet and some weirdo's still chuck out shit parcels.

   Once breakfast has been served or not as the case may be, the prisoners go to work. All adult male prisoners are required by law to work. That is a laugh, due mainly to overcrowding but also to the laziness of some prisoners there is massive unemployment within the prisons. That's not my concern here though; I want to look at the lighter side. So half the prisoners go to work and the rest are locked up. Work starts at about 09:00 and finishes at about 11:00. During that morning session, officers have to carry out certain tasks or duties. These include sorting, censoring and sealing the con's mail. Doing the L.B.B's. This is prison speak for checking all the Lock's Bolts and Bars of every cell on the wing. It's a monotonous time consuming job when done properly but it is bread and butter basic security and must be done. Also each day at least one prisoner and his cell are searched thoroughly. The con is picked at random by security and each con should expect to be searched every few months. If you ask any con about searching though, they will tell you they are always being picked on. That they only had a search a couple of days ago and they have nothing to hide but if you find anything it's not theirs and they know nothing about it.

Reports have to be written almost daily. Each officer is assigned six or eight prisoners and any paperwork coming in appertaining to any of those prisoners should be done as soon as possible. Some lifer reports are very time consuming and can take many hours to research and compile. It is very difficult to find the time in the day to do these reports as no facility time is granted to do them due to staff shortages.

Incoming mail must be sorted and dished out. Exercise is at 11:30. All prisoners are entitled to half an hour's exercise a day. This is taken on the yard and can be a dodgy place to be. Drugs are rife throughout the prison system and a lot of the deals are done on the yard. Attacks are common place. Mainly because this is the only place where all the con's from all the wings have a chance to meet. If someone has a grudge against someone else, he can find him and fight him on the yard. Working in this area can be tense.

At 11:45 dinner is served. This is a joyous occasion as prisoners have the choice from a wide and varied menu. They have five choices at lunchtime and an amazing six choices at tea. I think on the whole that the food is pretty good and I think that most staff would agree. The con's call it slop. And here is another unanswered question. Why do cons choose food they don't want? They get to choose their food a couple of weeks in advance. That's just the way it works. That gives them plenty of time to work out what they like. But you can virtually guarantee that when they come in for their food they will spot something else that looks better than the choice they have made, then will swear blind that they didn't choose it and the staff who wrote out the numbers must have made a mistake! They do it all the time. So much does this happen that we have to keep a record of everything ordered so we can prove them wrong. They can have their choice, have nothing or wait to the end and see what is left.

Dinner served (thankfully) then it's time for bang up. They are all locked in their cells at about 12:15 so staff can go to lunch at 12:30, although, one member of staff must stay on patrol on the wing throughout the dinner period.

At 13:45 it is time for round two and the whole process is pretty much repeated. We don't do the L.B.B's again and no more searching. Other duties around the prison include manning the visits hall, patrolling the corridors, patrolling the workshops and supervising the bin party (rubbish collectors).

At 16:30 the prisoners return from the workshops again where they are banged up by 17:00 for another half-hour or so for staff tea. The con's tea is then served and they are left open for what we call association. This is where the con's can relax downstairs on the wing and indulge in games of pool or table tennis and could watch T.V. or videos. Since the introduction of in cell T.V's there doesn't seem to be the same interest in the T.V. room as there used to be. They can also visit the prison library, go to the Gym, take part in education classes or go to the chapel. This culminates with my favourite part of the day, evening bang up at 20:15. The cons will collect water in flasks at this time ready for the long night. Another strange phenomenon takes place at this time. They all suddenly have to see everybody else before they bang up. Not satisfied with seeing each other all day. Never thinking forward that they might want to borrow something from a friend or get some tea bags because they have run out, go and get a bit of tobacco from someone, borrow a book or a paper or secure some drugs to take. They seem to cram all of these things into the final two minutes of the day. This ritual is carried out in every prison every night. And all the while staff are chasing round trying to get them in their respective cells. Follow this routine for 365 days and you will more or less have a prison year.

Of course there are changes from time to time. Incidents occur regularly. Staff shortages often mean curtailed regimes. A couple of wings may be banged up all evening, that kind of thing. But on the whole, that is all there is to look forward to on most days.

Bear all this in mind when you read this book. These incidents are the things that get us through the year. We never know when the next amusing or scary, challenging event will happen, but when it does it lifts the spirits. It boosts the staff morale. It even strengthens the bond between staff and prisoners, because the one thing that unites us all is laughter. Even the most challenging of incidents can unite the staff as they have to rely on each other to do their job without prompting from anyone else, and tackle whatever awful and usually, blood covered problem that presents itself. Amazingly humour can be found even in the most dreadful of these incidents.

I would like to pass on my thanks to all the people that have made this book possible, especially all the staff that have unwittingly passed on their stories over the years for inclusion here. Finally to all the "Smith's" and "Jones's" that have been involved in some of the funniest things I have ever witnessed. Cheers.

Cus'turd!

There are countless fights and arguments between staff and prisoners in the Servery. I blame the kitchens. An Army marches on its stomach, so the saying goes, prisoners continually whinge about theirs. Food is very important and plays a large part of prison life. Anything between a few hundred and a thousand cons will expect to be fed three times a day, with up to five different choices for the lunch and tea meal. That's a better choice than some of the more dubious hotels I've stayed in over the years. The only downside is the very meagre budget the kitchen staff have to work with. This is definitely not the Savoy we are talking about. Money is always tight, and corners are always being trimmed. They do their best but with little to work with, results are often poor. The days when no complaints are made are very few and far between.

 The worst thing is that the kitchen staff are not the ones that have to serve the stuff to the cons. They are never present when these culinary delights are dished up to the starving masses. It's amazing how everyone turns into Egon Ronay as the food is received; they dissect and digest every morsel before telling the staff how crap it is. The most common descriptive word used is "Slop", but it is rarely that bad! Yeah, the ones who take the flack are the wing staff. The kitchen boys can relax when they have burnt the pies. Why rush round trying to cook more? All they need do is send them to the wing without a word of apology, knowing the wing staff will do their utmost to bullshit their way through. They'll stand and lie through their teeth, telling the cons how good it is, arguing with those who try to refuse their meal, then tell them there is nothing else, so like it or lump it.

 Mind you, burnt pies are one thing but you should see the peas. Always full of bright green dye and Unidentified Floating Black Bits, or U.F.B.B's as I affectionately know them. I once saw the recipe for prison peas and it was as follows,

1) Take a huge sack of reasonable quality peas.
2) Boil them for as long as time will permit to remove as much flavour and colour as possible.
3) Add artificial flavour.
4) Add artificial colour.
5) Scrape around the kitchen floor and collect as many bits as possible and add them.
6) If enough bits cannot be found, open a sachet of regulation prison U.F.B.B's and add them instead.
7) Keep warm for hours until set and serve in unequal sized slices.

 The peas and their U.F.B.B's are always guaranteed to cause a good conflict, usually culminating in the whole tray being launched at high velocity across the hotplate, directed at whoever was serving them. This was usually the "Sprogg", the officer on the wing with the least time in, the older officers, usually having worn their fair share of peas through the years, happy to initiate the unsuspecting Servery virgin. Once you had been hit by flying peas, which rendered a new uniform useless, as the industrial strength artificial colouring stain would never come out you took every precaution to keep out of any future firing line.

There are of course many other regular culinary disasters, far too many to mention here but I feel I should let you in on a few of the classics.

Square Egg is up there in the top five of culinary catastrophe classics. This is pallid yellow in colour, blancmange in consistency, cut into squares and completely devoid of any eggy flavour. The only reason we call it square egg is because it is made with water and egg powder, with a lot of emphasis on the water. It would be hard to serve something called square water, so it is square egg! The egg powder is probably some genetically modified, manmade, chicken pip substitute that the home office has brought from one of its chemical warfare development laboratories during the cold war. It is absolute shite! No one ever eats it, and it always goes back to the kitchen completely untouched only to rear its ugly head a week or so later. I conducted my own experiment one summer and scribed my name in the back of a slice and popped it back into the tray. I was able to read my name sixteen times by Christmas..........when it was finally served up under the guise of Yorkshire Pudding!!

Cheesy Egg Beano is another prison speciality. Cooked fresh this Toast, Baked Bean, Fried Egg and Cheese combo would be a tasty treat, just a bit on the lardy side. Once the kitchen have got their hands on it, over cooked it, and left it to ferment in a hot trolley for a couple of hours, it metamorphosis's into a congealed, snotty cocktail, possibly only suitable for consumption by the pigs on the local farm where all the waste food went. The pigs would rather give you a bite than eat this rubbish! Mind you so would a lot of the cons during any struggle that may occur after the weekly serving of Beanos.

Highly skilled professionals and a load of cons operate the kitchens. The wing, from which these cons are selected, can also have a large bearing on how the food is cooked.

Some prisons contain "Main Stream" prisoners and "Nonce's". Mainstream cons are on what we call "Normal Location". These have committed all the usual crimes, like robbery, burglary, assault, drug possession and dealing etc. They can be held together as they are all as bad as each other. A nonce is a prisoner who is in for a sexually motivated crime and is viewed by most of the prison population as being very dodgy. Dispersed in amongst them, are the poor unfortunates that are tarred with the same nonce brush. These include cons that have asked for protection from the bullies, Cons that have grassed on others, Cons that have settled down and just want an easy life away from the hassles of the normal wings. Lastly, the poor inadequate's, who through no fault of their own, are of low intelligence or are too mentally unstable to cope on normal location. Oh, and really odd looking and ugly cons. Because they are all housed on the same wing, they are all branded as nonce's, regardless of their personal reasons for being there, and are fair game to normal cons. Abuse and assaults are commonplace if these two groups come into contact. In fact a large percentage of normal cons consider it their born duty, their only aim in life, to kick the shit out of a nonce at any opportunity.

Obviously it is the officer's duty to keep these two parties apart, and most of the time they do quite well. So other ways must be found by the normal's to get at their prey. Picture if you will a kitchen full of normal's, cooking for three wings full of nonce's. It's a recipe for disaster.

I had heard horror stories that I dismissed as prison myth about cons masturbating into the food and I didn't believe it. Mind you I never ate the food either. Well not from the nonce's end anyway! I'm sure there was a lot of selective serving going on as well.

"Bollocks I've burnt the pies".

"Fuck it. Give it to the nonce's" would be a common response often heard in prison kitchens throughout the country. I knew it went on, but it never bothered me. Someone had to eat it. The nonce's rarely complained. So it was never hard to fob them off with the bad food. Merrily they would march through the Servery with their plates or trays in hands, catching whatever was dolloped in their direction, always with a thank you and a happy glow that they were being well looked after.

On this particular day Jones was on the hotplate with an assortment of cons and officers. He was serving the custard. He was the more senior of the officers so pulled rank and put himself I/C (in charge) of custard serving duties, as it was generally an easy job to do. One ladle per bowl, it was as simple as that. Plus it was very popular so rarely attracted complaints. Bear in mind, there was three wings to serve with an average of 88 cons per wing. So there was a fuck off big vat of custard. Things were going swimmingly. The cons were wandering through in their usual sheep like manner. The view from behind the hotplate was great. It was like when the circus comes to town. Big ones, small ones, fat, thin and some with unusual deformities, many just normal looking but with very dark secrets, all taking their food blissfully unaware of the monster of the deep. Having served the first hundred or so portions, Jonesy could safely assume that the men at the head of the queue would have already eaten their food. They will have eaten their dinner then tucked into delicious sponge and custard, before settling down for an hour's kip, as cons do over lunch. By the time he'd served the second wing full, he was getting closer to the bottom of the custard vat, happy in the knowledge that many more would be settling down for their kip with full and satisfied bellies. Half way through the third wing, Jones began to get the feeling you get when you know something is not right. When you realise all is not as it should be. He got the nasty niff of poo that you wouldn't usually associate with a nice clean Servery. He carried on ladling and the smell got stronger. Other people noticed it too. No one said anything but there was tell tale signs. Noses twitching, heads turning, that kind of thing. Then BANG! Well more like a squish really, there was the culprit. Jonesy didn't see it straight away; as he was looking around to see if he could spot what he thought was a phantom farter.

"Fucking hell Gov. What the fuck is that!?"

Jonesy was standing mid-scoop, with ladle at head height, so as to extricate the next portion from the vat and there, half on and half off the cup of the ladle was the biggest turd you have ever seen. He immediately dropped it back in, ladle and all and slammed the lid down tight hoping no one else had noticed it. What was he thinking? You couldn't bloody miss it! As it rose from the depths, it brought with it a smell that permeated the whole hotplate area in the blink of an eye, or more accurately, the twitch of a nostril. Jones reddened, knowing what he had just done. Not dropping the thing back in no, that was the right thing to do given the circumstances. It was the realisation that he had just served three hundred people with sponge, shit and custard that upset him.

"Custards off!" Jones shouted so the rest of the queue could hear. The cons in line in the immediate vicinity didn't need to be told. But those tail enders that were lucky enough to be out of the sniff zone were mortified.

"We want our custard Gov," They moaned.

"Oh no you don't!" Jonesy retorted, but it fell on deaf ears.

"Come on Gov. We want custard," came the chants.

"No you fucking don't. Now piss off," snapped Jonesy. But their insistence was relentless. Most of them disbursed, leaving only a handful of die-hard custard addicts all desperate for their fix, and they refused to budge.

"Alright" says Jonesy, removing the lid and lifting the ladle, "Have a look at that bastard!"

Off they scurried, gagging as they left, all except for one particularly persistent and horrible little nonce, who was very wrinkled with a squinty eye. He pointed at the brown and yellow submarine and said,

"Just flick that in the bin Gov. I can't miss me custard!"

Follow That Bus

"That's where we're going, just follow us", was probably one of the most regrettable things Jonesy had ever uttered.

Jones had been in the job for several years. He followed in his proud father's footsteps. Well known for his exhausting sense of humour and never ending jovial antics, he was a well-liked officer with many friends in the service. People were always waiting to see what stupid thing Jones would do next. In his early thirties, short and carrying a bit of extra weight, although still fit, he was Mr. Average officer apart from his jester like qualities.

On the day in question, he had been detailed the Onley Run. HMP Onley was used as a sort of prisoner distribution centre. It was like going to cons-are-us. All the prisons in the area would arrive with their respective cons, that all had pre arranged transfers. They would all be held in holding cells, fed and watered, then taken back to their new prisons after all the swapping had been completed. The escorting staff simply had to check the identities of the incoming cons and take them back. The hardest and sometimes most worrying part of the day was checking for the warrants. Every convicted prisoner should have a warrant in his file. This is the proof that he has been convicted and must be present for him to legally be held within the confines of the prison. You would have thought that such an important document would have a special pouch or pocket within the folder to aid easy access. But on almost every visit to this prisoner warehouse, frantic moments were spent scrambling through reams of paperwork trying to find this golden ticket. Worried staff from all the visiting establishments would panic uncontrollably until the thing was found. All knowing full well that all the assembled cons had all been in for some time so would obviously have a warrant present. If the warrant was not present, the transfer could not take place and the con had grounds for immediate release. So you can see why the staff would worry if it was not found. I don't know of an occasion when a warrant wasn't eventually located.

 The searching for this document on most occasions went like this;

Officer one would casually leaf through the folder and not find the warrant saying, "It's not here."

Officer two would then take over and look through the folder having called officer one a Pratt for not finding it and would also say; "It's not here!"

Officer three would then look through the file after officer two had also failed in his search, while calling both his friends wanker's, then say, "It's not here!"

Officer one would now rifle through the folder again after snatching it back from the completely incompetent officer three, while yelling "It's not here, it's not fucking here!"

Officer two, by this time, would be snatching at any bit of paperwork he could grab from the folder to double check his previous check, now fearing he would lose his job.

Officer three would be trying to calm the situation by screaming at the others that they must have lost it or dropped it and would initiate his second search, shouting "It's not fucking here!!"

At this point an officer from another prison would casually stroll past and would point at the warrant sticking out of the semi-demolished folder and say "There it is."

The very same officer would then return to his friends and the whole dramatic affair would start again within a different group!

On arrival at HMP Onley all staff were given a job for the duration of their visit. There was only a handful of full time staff working in this area, so staff from other jails manned almost the whole interchange operation. This caused a few problems when most of the staff on a particular day had never been before. There were some really riveting jobs I can tell you. "Manning the coach park" was a classic. This involved unlocking and locking a gate to let waiting coaches into a fenced area. "Main Gate" was another beauty, which involved unlocking and locking the gate to the interchange compound. The worst was "Manning the cells". This included feeding the cons, letting them out for the loo and checking I.D's which would have been cool if you were dealing with normal cons in their usual surroundings, but these were cons on escort. These turned into argumentative, objectionable arseholes that would do anything to piss you off. There must be some prisoner manual somewhere that explains to the prison virgin, how to behave in certain prison based situations.

I imagine it would say,

1. On escort do the exact opposite of what you're told!
2. Ask for the toilet as many times as possible.

3. Try to go back to any cell other than the one you came out of.
4. No matter how good the food is, tell the screws you don't like it, or tell them you have a doctor's note which says you can't eat it. (Most cons have a doctor's note for something).
5. Always scream in pain when the nice officer gently and carefully applies the handcuffs to your wrists.
6. Do your best to get on the wrong vehicle.
7. Try to be sick, preferably in transit.

The whole affair was organised chaos but it always seemed to work. Though thankfully, since the introduction of private companies taking over all the escorts, the Interchange has closed down.

Jonesy was busy sorting through all the relevant forms and paperwork on this particular morning. He had been tasked by the Senior Officer to do all the running around, as often happens in situations such as this, when there is work to be done. The person in charge will delegate then sit on their arse drinking tea. Mind you if anything went wrong, the shit would always fall on the head of the I/C (in charge) officer, and that was usually the S.O. It was his right to drink tea, as he would have to catch the poo if it fell.

Jonesy carried out his duties and was ready to leave. The prisoners that matched his paperwork had been collected and loaded onto the bus. The escorting staff were in their seats as Jonesy collected all the keys together and took them into the gate as they left. In the gate he heard someone ask the question,

"Do you know the way to HMP Onley?"
He didn't look up as he uttered that disastrous answer,
"That's where we're going, just follow us!"
The question had come from a visiting probation officer.
Having seen his morning client he was now on his way to
his afternoon appointment which happened to be at HMP
Onley. He couldn't believe his luck. He had never been
to Onley before. These staff were going there and all he
had to do was follow the bus.

John was a tall muscular Rastafarian. A probation officer
for years, he enjoyed his job and lived well on his wages.
The bright red new BMW (or Beamer as they are known)
he was driving would have prompted many people to
think he was on the wrong side of the law. He fitted
perfectly into the awful stereotype of a drug dealer, black
male, dreadlocks, dripping in gold and driving a
convertible Beamer. He would be the first to admit he
looked a bit suspect but he enjoyed playing up to the part.
As the coach left he ran to his car, jumped in and pulled
in behind the coach ready for the hour long journey.

The coach had already visited a couple of other prisons
during the morning. It was full as usual and the next stop
was the interchange at Onley. Jonesy sat at the back
acting up and telling jokes like a schoolboy on an outing.
He always livened up the boring journey and today
would be no exception.
Bob the driver had travelled this route far too many times
to count. He was very experienced and had done more
courses than you could shake two sticks at. You see,
transporting prisoners involved a lot more than just
driving. Security was one of the main concerns. There

was a constant risk of possible escape attempts from either within the vehicle or assisted from the outside. Although the cons were all cuffed, the high percentage of cons to officers heightened the risk and the driver needed to be vigilant.

After only a couple of miles, Bob spotted a flash BMW following the bus close behind. Nothing to unusual he thought but when he got a closer look and spotted a Rasta covered in gold his suspicions were raised. He continued on his route and started to get positively worried when the Beamer jumped a set of lights to stay in touch with the bus.

"Shit we're being followed", thought Bob to himself as he continued along his pre-planned route. It was time to test his suspicions. Instead of going straight over the next roundabout, he indicated right and doubled back on himself along the dual carriageway he had just travelled. Sure enough, there in the wing mirror was the red Beamer. He turned right again and re-traced his route back to the previous roundabout and there he was again. "Shit", thought Bob. "This is real. I'll try something else".

He looked for a narrow side street that was well off the beaten track and drove down that. This was not such a good idea as the coach could only just squeeze through and the Beamer followed with ease. If there was going to be an attempt to take the bus that would have been an ideal opportunity and Bob chastised himself for his foolishness. He was sure now though that the Beamer was ready to assist in an escape attempt and reported his fears to the Senior Officer.

Some of the more experienced officers on the bus were also becoming a little suspicious. They had noticed the double back and wondered why the hell the driver almost got the bus stuck down the narrow side street.

In the meantime, John the Rasta was losing his rag.

"Where the fuck is this guy going?" he cursed to himself, "Is he lost?"

Patiently though he followed. Up and down dual carriageways, round roundabouts and down alleys.

"What's he doing man? He can't be lost!? I should have just found my own way man!"

Jonesy the officer had been oblivious. He was in the middle of one of his jokes when he first realised something was up. He kept seeing the tops of officer's heads peeping up over the tops of their seats, trying to get a view out the back of the bus of the potential escape party.

"What they looking at me for? What have I done now?" Jonesy thought to himself. He tried to ignore them but got nervous when the looks continued.

Bob continued with his circular route, waiting for the S.O. to decide their next move.

"Jesus Christ" shouted John the Rasta to himself, "I can hardly keep up with this madman. Where the hell are they going man?"

Jonesy realised there was something definitely going on. The whispers among the staff finally made their way to the back of the bus.

"There's a possible escape attempt going on!" Jones was told.

"What the fuck? How do you know? What's going on?"

"The guy in the BMW behind us" Jonesy was told. His palms became instantly sweaty. He slowly turned round, ducking slightly so as not to be spotted by the escape party and there was a familiar face behind the wheel of the Beamer. Jonesy caught the eye of the driver behind them and was greeted with a friendly but weary wave. Officers' heads slowly turned to look at Jonesy who was by now as red as a Lobsters arse.

The colour soon drained from Jonsey's cheeks though as the realisation of what he had done started to sink in. "Fuck it!" he thought "No one will know it was me" but his embarrassment was too hard to hide. Not as hard to hide as the honking horn and flashing lights coming from the escape party's car as John tried to attract the attention of his new friend.

"Do you know that guy?" a voice said from somewhere within the bus.

"NO!" snapped Jones, "He's nothing to do with me!"

"Well he keeps waving every time you look round!"

"Whys that bastard keep ignoring me!?" John shouted out loud, "What's going on?"

As he said this, he made his move to try to draw next to the bus so he could make contact with the shrinking figure in the back seat.

The S.O. took this as the move he had been dreading, the escape attempt was about to be made. The BMW was now next to the bus, horn blasting and lights flashing. The S.O. was sure it was trying to force the bus to stop. There was only one thing for it. He picked up the emergency phone and dialled 999. As the signal was being beamed to distant satellites, Jonesy launched himself from his place of safety and hurtled down the aisle of the bus to try to intercept the outgoing signal. As

he went into a kind of slow motion he shouted
"NOooooooooooo"
The S.O. shit himself as he thought the potential escapee
was making his move.
Jonesy grabbed the phone and said "It was me! I told him
to follow the bus. He's a probation officer going to
Onley!"
"Are you taking the piss you complete and utter
fucking...........................?"
I'll leave it there for you to fill in the rest yourself. Mark
my words, whatever you fill in; it will be nowhere near
as bad as the original. Needless to say Jonesy had a lot of
explaining to do that day.

Our Best Cleaner

Smith had only been on the wing about a week and Officer Jones was fast becoming concerned. There was something about the con that bothered him but he just couldn't put his finger on it.

He was a thin stick of a man, who rarely shaved and had rotted teeth. There was a smell that accompanied him wherever he went, an unnerving smell that was like a cross between stale piss and death. He was also covered in scars. I mean his head was just really covered in scars. It was like looking at a Braille book full of head injuries. You could almost read that this guy had been through wars, he'd seen some action but he didn't look like your average scrapper. You could usually tell who liked a fight. They would come on to the wing full of bravado, puffing up their chests and giving everybody the look. You know that look that a person who thinks, or worse still, knows they are hard, gives out that says I'm here look at me, don't cross me or you'll get it. Smith didn't have this look. He was a skinny little runt who wouldn't want to fight his way out of a wet paper bag through fear of injury but he had the scars.

Well if he wasn't a fighter, then he must be a victim. He must have been so badly bullied and abused over the years that his head now looked like a sad and badly beaten old punch bag, but why? What had he done to deserve it? For no other reason, other than morbid fascination Jonesy thought he would try to find out.

Most of the time you can get a pretty good rapport going with any con as long as you try putting yourself out a bit. There is always an angle that will get you in. Even for the most hardened of convicts. The ones that would completely blank any staff member and would carry on as if you were their worst enemy. There would always be something that he would want, sooner or later, and if you can deliver that thing, then you were in. You were the one that would be trusted. You would build the relationship and be the one to help the guy out. No one could do this was Smith. He was like a self-contained unit, a closed shop. He asked for nothing, wanted nothing, did nothing. He went nowhere, spoke to no one, and never got involved. He was always so vacant. All those funny sayings that you hear about mad or weird people were all made up about him. You know the kind I mean. "A sandwich short of a picnic" "The lights are on but there's no one home" That kind of thing. Well his lift definitely did not go to the top floor! Jonesy really was struggling, he had never met an egg as hard to crack as this one before.

The days and weeks passed and Smiths impressive collection of bodily injuries consistently grew. His head was ever changing like the passing of the seasons. There was always an impressive array of colours and bumps and often-open cuts.
Jonesy would ask him directly,
"Who has hit you Smith? What has happened to you?" But time and again he would shrug his shoulders and walk off. It was time to do some digging.
Jonesy got on well with a few of the cons on this wing, so thought he'd be able to find out what was happening. After asking around, he had still drawn a blank. Smith was such a private bloke Jonesy was told that no one knew anything about him.

It was quite by chance that one day Jonesy found some tablets while conducting a cell search. (Cells were searched daily and any items that shouldn't be in there were removed. If there were no good reasons why the occupant had the item, he would find himself in front of the governor to receive a punishment of some kind.)

Jonesy had not come across these tablets before and thought it best to check them out. He was surprised to find they had originally belonged to Smith. They were Epilepsy tablets. Officers are not at liberty to find out about a man's medical records. Only the Health Care staff had access to those. That's why he had not seen this coming. He didn't think for a second that the strange behaviour Smith was displaying was linked to an illness or medical condition. But what were his tablets doing in somebody else's cell? and if Smith was on tablets to control his fits, why was he so bashed up? Jonesy assumed that falling over all the time had caused his injuries, but the tablets should be controlling that. He had a word with the con that was in possession of the tablets. After listening to loads of bullshit and cutting a deal with the guy that he wouldn't find himself in front of the Governor, for having someone else's stuff, he finally admitted that he had bought them off Smith for a phone card. Phone Cards used to be one of the main currencies in prison*. As most people use the phones all the time, cards are used in much the same way as notes outside, except they only come in the £2 variety. So whatever is being sold has to be divided up into combinations of 2. All the Heroin addicts would but £10 deals for 5 phone cards; they could get a blowjob from the resident queer for 10 phone cards and so on. Quite what sort of a kick anyone would get from Smith's Epilepsy tablets was

never established but at least now it was known why
Smith looked like a crash test dummy.

 The word was spread and the Health Care informed.
Keep an eye on Smithy, he's flogging his tabs, and was
very likely to injure himself continuously if he carried on
doing so. The staff tried to stop him, and he kept saying
he wouldn't do it anymore but still he kept on crashing
down. The trouble was, and this is the reason why no one
ever saw him fall, he had always been locked up during
the day, as he had no job. (The unemployment was high
at this prison and only the most enthusiastic managed to
secure a job.) So any skull cracking fits he had were all
behind closed doors. He kept himself to himself in the
evenings preferring not to associate with the others
downstairs. He stayed in his cell and generally banged up
early. How had the staff missed it? They decided the best
thing they could do was give him a job on the wing as a
cleaner. That way they could keep a close eye on him and
monitor the frequency of his fits and establish whether or
not he was selling his much-needed tablets.
 Well it was worse than they thought.
 He readily accepted the job and happily started on
Monday morning with the others. He lasted a good hour
before the officer's heard an almighty crash and there
laid Smith in the bucket and broom cupboard shaking
like the leaves on a tree. Having had previous experience
of this, Officer Jones made him comfortable by putting
something soft under his head, kept him warm with a
blanket and moved all the other inanimate objects away
so as to reduce the risk of injury. Twenty minutes or so
later he finally came round with yet another whopper of a
lump to add to his amazing collection. Tuesday came and

Smiths second day started in much the same way. This time he was mid way between the first and second step up to the 1's when he keeled over for the second time and started his increasingly familiar floorshow. This time he had luckily avoided hitting his head but had managed to open up a rather impressive gash near his elbow, which required stitching. Was there no limit to this man's talents?

Wednesday morning was non-eventful and staff were optimistic that he could get through the day, but the afternoon let them down. Half in and half out of their very busy office, Smith went down and blocked the doorway for a good half-hour and they were starting to regret their decision to take Smith on.

Jonesy asked one of the nurses how often he should be fitting, and she said not at all if he was taking his medication. As much as they tried to talk him round he wouldn't stop selling it.

Thursday saw another big crash, followed by a fifth in so many days on Friday, all with bone shattering consequences. This was getting stupid. Staff were getting pissed off going to his rescue and all the other cleaners were getting fed up of looking out for him. What made it worse for them was that staff were always on the landings keeping an eye out. There was always loads for staff to do and they had no spare time to watch out for Smith, but to try to limit his crashes, one of them would spend a lot of time patrolling the landings to keep an eye on him. This meant that the other cleaners would have to keep themselves busy, as they would also be under constant scrutiny. They preferred to be left to their own devices so plenty of skiving could be done. Of course they weren't happy about being watched and this all came down to Smith. It wasn't long before the cleaners got their own back and the staff got one hell of a laugh.

 Now in his second week as a cleaner and still fitting regularly, Smith was working on the first landing. With hindsight, this was a bit of a dodgy decision for the officers to make. Things were going well but the staff were all tied up in their work and had no time to run around after Smith. His first few tell tale wobbles had gone unnoticed and before long the inevitable happened. The first they knew about it was when they heard a loud shout coming from the stairwell.

"Gov, you had better come and look at this" called a loud and worried voice. A pensive head was shoved out of the office door but nothing was seen in the direction of the shout. A scout was sent out on a mission to discover the reason for the alarm and was met with a fantastic sight. There at the bottom of the stairs was Smith in his usual position. Not just lying there, no, this was much better. Surrounded by buckets and mops, Smith was lying face down with his arms and legs outstretched. Carefully placed under the end of each limb was a wooden scrubbing brush. Also there was about a bucket full of strong cleaning fluid spread all over the floor in his immediate vicinity. Unbeknown to Smith he was scrubbing like he had never scrubbed before. His usual thrashing, which tended to be quite vigorous, was being assisted by the lubrication the cleaning fluid was adding, and by goodness the floor was coming up a treat.

 The cleaners had got their own back. Fed up with having to watch over him and pick him up every time he fell, they decided to teach him a lesson he wouldn't forget.

Mind you, there was just one flaw to that plan. Smith never remembered anything after a fit, but that was just a minor detail. This was just pretty to watch.

 Five minutes after the staff found him, Smith had got this section of the floor really clean. This may sound cruel, but not wanting to miss an opportunity, rather than get out the usual pillow and blanket, they just slid him along in the ever-increasing foam and had him do the next bit! He was working like a trooper. At this rate he would qualify for a bonus, such was the sterling job he was doing. There was a particularly nasty stain in a hard to get to corner, so five minutes later they manoeuvred this half man half deep cleaning machine into a new position so his left foot was firmly jammed into the corner. His left leg always seemed to get a bit more of a whip on than the other limbs, so was the perfect tool for the job. It came up a treat. This was great.

The wing had one of those circular electric stripping and polishing machines but that was boring compared to this. Plus, because of its circular motion, it would never reach right into the corners. Smith did. Once that stubborn stain was gone, the officers became more ambitious. With a bit more lubrication and a lot more vigorous shaking they actually got him to self-propel. They didn't even have to move him manually and all the area was being covered with Smith on auto-pilot! The joke had gone better than anyone could have hoped.

 When he finally came round he had done the whole of the stairwell entrance, and what a great job he'd done too. The roars of laughter from upstairs gave away the other cleaners viewing position, but by now it didn't matter. The deed had been done and justice was served. Smith had got his comeuppance at last. All the aggravation the cleaners and the officer's had been through was now repaid.

 Smith was none the wiser. He couldn't work out why he was so wet and slimy, and there was a noticeable change to his aroma. "Clean" was a condition Smith had long forgotten, but he was pretty chuffed with this re-introduction. Once told what had happened, he really made the effort to change his ways. He found it very hard to hide his embarrassment and promised to shape up. He took his tablets, stopped his fitting and became the wings best cleaner.

* Many prisons now have a Pin Phone system, which is run on a credit buying method. All the calls are made using pre-paid credit, to numbers on a pre-submitted list; thus removing the ability for cons to use phone cards as currency.

Arse Star

Smith was a normal looking guy as far as prisoners go. A few scars, usually unshaven, normal build and pretty quiet but there was a sinister, darker side to him that seldom reared its ugly head. Staff were very aware of his dangerous abilities and would avoid being alone with him if they knew what was good for them.

The murder of another prisoner was a very serious crime but it meant much more to the staff that were now in charge of this man. He didn't give a shit about anyone or anything. He had committed the ultimate in the prison world, (killing a fellow prisoner) and to everyone around him; this made him a very dangerous bastard indeed.

Coupled with these psychopathic tendencies, was the fact that he was an extreme self harmer.

Self harming is a well known phenomenon throughout the prison system, but was something Officer Jones had not come across before he joined the service. Only employed for 6 months or so, he had seen more slashing and cutting than you could shake a razor at. The prison he worked in was full of very troubled prisoners and had more than its fair share of slasher's.

There are a few reasons for this harming. Some prisoners do it as a cry for help. I know that's not very politically correct, but there really are some guys that will scratch themselves just so they get plenty of attention from the staff. They could be depressed and low or are having trouble coping with some emotional trauma, like a death in the family or a partner leaving etc. They just want attention from someone. They don't know how to ask for help or rather won't ask. Any attention is good attention

and as long as someone notices, job done!
Others do it as a release. They don't want anyone to
know. They will slash behind closed doors and usually
staff will only know when they spot some semi healed
scars. Then there are the out and out mental sods, like
Smithy in this story.

Most self harm takes the form of some kind of cutting
somewhere on the body, usually with an open razor
blade. Most prison wings hand out bic safety razors but
these can be easily opened to reveal the blade inside.
Mind you, I've witnessed some pretty horrific injuries
when people have actually tried to shave with these
cheap and very crappy razors.
You can usually gauge the seriousness or desperation of
the prisoner by the depth and direction of the cuts they
make. A hundred light scratches directly across the wrist
with hardly any bloodletting, is a pretty poor effort and
really means, talk to me please. Where as a single long,
deep gash down the full length of the inner wrist, where
blood hits the ceiling is a serious problem. Not only to
the owner of the wrist or the hospital staff trying to sew
the veins and re-attach the ligaments and tendons but also
to the poor wing cleaning officer who will have to try to
secure some paint to re-decorate the cell from the prison
store man. Incidentally, they are a strange breed who
believe they have a job as a store man as things are
supposed to be stored. If they were supposed to issue
stuff, they would be called an issue man!

In Jonesy's short service he had seen some very serious
self assaults. One guy opened up his wrists in his first
week. On entering the cell he found a scene resembling a

horror movie with hardly a blood free surface in the cell. Various minor attempts followed, where a lot of scratchers did their best to express their desperation. Jonesy even witnessed the prison legend they call "Zippy". So called because he had cut open his stomach so often that the flesh and skin had died and now all that held his guts in place was a kind of clear plastic sheet. Now when ever Zippy got upset, he would simply walk into the wing office and pull off the sheet to spill his guts out all over the officer's desk. Staff were so used to this though it was nothing unusual. It would be,
"Oh fucking hell Zippy! No!!. Someone bring a mop, this dick heads dropped his guts again!!"

But Smith was different. His was an evil self mutilation that Jonesy never witnessed again for the rest of his service.
The staff knew Smith could be volatile and should be watched. Indeed, he was a Category "A" prisoner and needed to be watched as a matter of course. Every now and again though, he would go into a deep depression and would walk around like a zombie. Staff would only walk around in two's at these times. He had already shown his capabilities by killing the other prisoner and no one wanted to risk being his next victim.
It was during one of these particularly dark periods that Jonesy was on duty on Smith's wing. He was aware of him but did not know Smith that well, as this was not his usual place of work. So it was strange that Smith approached Jonesy just before lock up and told him he didn't feel too good, and could he have a word with the officer later in his cell. Officer Jones reluctantly agreed and said he would go see him as soon as everyone was

locked up.

Ten minutes later with most of the cons away, Jonesy approached Smiths door, which was already locked. The locks on these doors were fitted with sprung loaded locks that would operate when pulled to or slammed shut. Jonesy shouted through the locked door, "Are you alright Smith?" but got no response.

"Are you OK?" he shouted again.

"Look through the spy hole", came the reply, which he did but could not see anything as the light was off. Jonesy used the light switch outside the cell but still could not make out what was going on within. It was just as he was about to shout again, that he looked down at his feet and the hairs instantly stood up on the back of his neck. In a cold sweat he stared down, eyes wide, at the pool of deep red blood that was rapidly forming around his feet.

 "Staff!!" he shouted at the top of his voice. (This is a well recognised call for help that any available staff, in earshot, will respond to.) For what seemed like hours but was only about 10 seconds, Jonesy stood motionless, frozen to the spot, waiting for his friends to come and help.

As the door snapped open, Jonesy snapped into action and darted into the cell to sort out whatever mess was on the other side of that door. The officers frantically searched the blood stained, naked body lying on the floor for the severe wounds that would be required to produce that much claret. Grabbing at his wrists, his neck, his groin and legs, they found nothing. They turned him over and searched again, nothing. Then Jonesy spotted something. A small white piece of plastic lodged between his blood spattered butt cheeks. In the panic and not really sure what he was grabbing, Jonesy pulled the plastic, which gave a lot of resistance and was shocked at what he revealed. This was the very end of the handle of a toothbrush. Whatever it was that had driven this man to such desperate measures was unknown but he had really done it in style. A quick rinse of the brush revealed that he had melted the bristle end of the brush with a flame. Into this molten plastic he had arranged and stuck six razor blades into a star shape to produce a very dangerous weapon. Then for reasons known only to him, Smith rammed this star shaped slashing tool up his arse, (actually right up into the hole) again and again, in fact maybe a hundred times until he became so week from either pain or blood loss, that he collapsed there in that sorrowful blood stained mess.

"Why?" was the only word uttered from one of Jonsey's blood stained colleagues.

The ambulance was called, although no one held out any hope for his survival. He was transferred to another prison nearby that had its own hospital wing. It was immediately apparent that the inadequately trained staff would not be able to deal with such severe trauma, but Smith was drifting off fast and needed to be stabilised before he was moved. Eventually, after losing him twice, and pumping copious amounts of blood into his veins and out of his arse, he was eventually taken to A & E.

He had lacerated virtually every single major organ that could be reached with an eight inch toothbrush. How the hell do you sew that? You don't! You just keep pouring blood in one end and hope it clots at the other. I think someone mentioned 40 pints as a rough estimate of the quantity that was needed that night. Did he survive? Of course he did, after much surgery and a nice new Gucci colostomy bag! He's probably still in the system somewhere, thanks to the rapid response of Jones and his boys. But, will their mental scars ever heal, from the atrocities they witnessed that night? I shouldn't think so!!

Electric Spoons

The decision had been made that all prisoners should have access to a toilet 24 / 7.

Up until this point, the only facilities most prisoners had during the night time lock up was a plastic pot or bucket in their cell. Bad enough in a single cell, but pretty awful when sharing with someone else. Urinating in a plastic pot was one thing but numbers twos? No way. Desperate means called for desperate measures and this bodily function was taken care of by the famous prison phenomenon, "The Shit Parcel" Every prison had them and there was a whole labour force employed country wide just to clear them up.

The con with the Turtle's Head would lie out a few sheets of his favourite paper, usually The Sun. Although in later years, that was superseded by The Sport, due to its sparkling array of classy models and incredibly believable news items. Also spotted was the odd copy of The Times, although this was considered very posh and was few and far between.

He would then squat over the paper and drop the bog monster onto the middle of the sheets. The essential paperwork would be done and dropped on top of the stinking heap. This would then be folded and wrapped much the same as with the technique employed in any local Chippy. Finally, it would be hoofed at high velocity, rather than just being dropped to the floor, either to the left or the right out of the con's window. This was done so that the guilty shitter could argue innocence, as there was not actually any crap outside his window. Mind you the con next door would use the same well-practiced technique, and they would end up getting each other in the shit, so to speak.

As you can imagine, the authorities frowned on this past time and would nick anyone who was caught practising it. All that crap needed picking up, so each wing would employ outside cleaners, affectionately known as the "Bomb Squad", to keep their areas clean.

So often were they out there poo picking, that they began to recognise the creator of each finely handcrafted package. Each con would have their own way of folding it. Also the size of it or the angle or distance of its trajectory, were all tell tale signs of the con that had given birth to this morning's collection of nasties.

Every now and again, a member of the bomb squad may upset someone else on the wing and a common way to get them back was to not properly seal their nightly deposits. You could tell if there had been a bit of a row between cleaner and thrower as the loosely packed bomb would have exploded on impact and spread over a wide fall out area. Instead of the usual scoop and slop with the shit shovel, more intense methods of cleaning would need to be employed using a broom and water.

As a new member of staff you were often placed in charge of the bomb squad, as it was a shit job and no one wanted it. When Jones first joined he made the mistake of commenting to the wing P.O. how he hated the parcel job and found himself on it for next 12 months until a new victim transferred in. Such was the mentality of some prison management.

So the news that toilet access would soon be provided was a relief to all.

Due to the size of the cells in this particular establishment, it was impossible to fit any kind of toilet and sink system into the tiny area left around the bed. It was an old series of buildings that wasn't originally built as a prison, and hand been redesigned some 30 odd years previous.

Over the preceding months prior to the work starting, various surveyors, architects, contractors and builders came and went until "A" wing was finally emptied of cons and work was started. Rumour had it that £5 million had been given to the Governor to pay for the work. The first team were brought in and contracted for £5 million. They immediately brought in a second team, gave them £4 million, pocketed a million and were never seen again. Not wanting to look a gift horse in the mouth, the second contactors subbed out to a third for £3 million and did a similar bunk with a similar million profit. Then a fourth were paid £2 million and finally a fifth contractor was paid £1 million and not a single stroke of work had been done up to this point. Of course as the pot got smaller and smaller, the quotes from the firms became tighter and tighter. The electronics and materials used became cheaper and crapper and I think that's where the problem began.

The work took months but eventually all five wings were fitted with one new sparkly clean toilet in the corner of each landing for the communal use of all housed on that landing. To enable the cons to have access to the new crapper, there was an accompanying electronic system that did a number of things.

1) Allowed each con to press a call button in their cell to electronically open their door to allow them access to the loo.
2) Allowed staff to talk to any cell via an intercom system.
3) Allowed staff to talk directly to any con out on the landing so they could be told to finish their business and return to their cell.
4) Allowed the con to lock himself back into his cell via a push button control panel within the cell.
5) Controlled an over ride system so all prisoner access to the toilet could be suspended, enabling night patrol staff access to the landing.

For a con to use the loo it worked like this. He would press the call button on the wall in his cell. This would put him in a queue. On his turn, the Nightsan computer would unlock his door. He then had 9 minutes to go about his business and return to his cell, once back in, he would peer with one eye into a small spy hole in the new control panel, where he would see a randomly generated 4-figure number. He would tap the digits into the control panel and hey presto the door would lock with the relieved con safely inside. The whole number thing was to ensure the con was actually in the cell and not just closing the door from the outside. The control panel was placed on the hinge side of the door to ensure the con could not see the numbers and lock himself out.

Time and again the long-suffering staff in the control room had to call out across the Tannoy for the con to return to his cell well after his 9 minutes were up. Seldom did they come out to use the loo but spent their 9 minutes wandering the landing, flitting from cell to cell passing all sorts of illicit items and talking to their mates. They were allowed out twice in one night and all made sure they well and truly abused the privilege.

Smith was nicknamed Bananaman. He was an unassuming, short, weak individual but had an IQ the size of the moon. He was a bank robber by trade who held up his chosen targets with his weapon of choice a Banana. This he would hide in a bag and fool the cashiers into thinking it was a gun. He thought he was doing no wrong as he was only pointing a Banana but the judge didn't see it that way and he received a long custodial. He had a lot of time to think about things and it wasn't long before his restless, inquisitive mind turned its attention to a new toy..........the Nightsan system.

While walking around the landing on one of his hourly patrols, the night cloggy, as they are affectionately known, was alerted by the sound of laughter coming from a cell. There were no T.V.'s in cells at this time, so due to the fact he could hear more than one laugh he quickly realised there was a serious problem. A quick, quiet peek through the spy hole confirmed his fears, as there were 4 cons in the cell, including Bananaman. The night cloggy was frozen to the spot, the door may open at any second and he could be attacked. He considered his options and finally managed to run to the landing door locking it shut behind him and immediately called for help. Backup arrived and the 4 cons were led away to the block still laughing. They could not see the seriousness of what they had done. After all, they were only playing cards.

 Three of these cons were swiftly transferred to other prisons and branded as escapees. But Bananaman was kept in the block, as he was the only one deemed clever enough to have worked something like this out. For weeks he remained tight lipped. Actually enjoying the mental challenge presented by the constant interviews and interrogations. He loved being the centre of attention. He wanted to let them know how clever he was but was enjoying the chase more. It wasn't until the staff decided to change tact and resorted to the old reverse psychology. They told him he was a thick twat, that could never have beaten that system, then he sung like a canary.

 He told them from start to finish exactly what he did but the staff didn't believe a word of it. So he told them again just the same as the first and the staff said, "Bollocks. Show us".

 So he did!

 Bananaman was led to his cell, which had remained sealed since he was removed from the wing, where he got all of his million pound system busting equipment together. This consisted of 5 plastic spoons, 5 screws and 5 bits of string, 2 mirrors and the lens from a national health pair of glasses.

Firstly he set up the 2 mirrors on his cell furniture, on angles, similar to that employed in a periscope, so he could look through the spy hole onto the mirror opposite. This in turn would reflect onto the other mirror in the other corner, which in turn would show the image of the control panel on the hinge side of the door. Over the small spy hole he placed the lens from his glasses, which would magnify any numbers needed to punch into the control panel to lock the door. With these items in position he could now see the numbers quite clearly from outside the cell. The pressing of the buttons was taken care of with the spoons, screws and string. All 5 spoons were placed between 2 thin pieces of wood, (stolen from the carpentry shop) and formed a lever system. Five small screws were turned into the bowl end of the spoons and the contraption was positioned over the control panel buttons using sticky tape. The string was tied to the handle ends of the spoons, and then fed through the gap between the door and the frame, which was about half an inch, so allowed an easy passage.

Bananaman then demonstrated his Nightsan Buster. He was locked into his cell and the Nightsan was activated. He pressed his call button and casually exited the cell and shut the door behind him. By looking through the spy hole he could see the magnified numbers on the control panel and took hold of the four strings. He pulled 1,2,3,4 and the door clicked shut. As far as the computer was concerned, he was locked in. The door was shut and he had pressed the right combination, so he was in. As he smugly grinned at the assembled Governors and security team, not to mention the contractors who installed the system, he coolly said,

"The Bananaman strikes again!" then almost pissed himself laughing.

The system allowed prisoners two visits to the toilet. There was no time limit between the two visits other than the time it took to for the usual queue. This of course allowed him the chance to re-enter his cell.

He then pulled the fifth string attached to the spoon over the call button. The door clicked open; he entered and started packing away his kit, as he had done for weeks. He was so well rehearsed at this he almost forgot the 12 pairs of eyes burning into him from the doorway.

"Smith SEG!" bellowed the security P.O. and he was marched off ready to prepare for his immanent escort to a Top Security prison the following day.

The Nightsan was immediately suspended. It was discovered, after frantic searching by wing staff, that almost every con on the wing had purchased a Nightsan Buster from the entrepreneurial Bananaman.

For about 12 months it remained suspended much to the disgust of the European Court of Human Rights, the Area Manager and the Prisons Ombudsman (who had to answer the hundreds of complaints), the Governor (who had his arse kicked by the above), the Contractors who had to come up with the solution, the staff who had to go out with the re-employed bomb squad and the bomb squad themselves, who had to cope with a massive resurgence of open parcels, as all the cons were protesting at losing their twice nightly walks around the landings.

The final solution was absolute rubbish. The contractors fitted an external metal beading around the inside of the frame. This stopped the strings from being fed through the gap, but made it almost impossible to open the door if the con barricaded up inside. They also fitted a blue tinted spy hole glass, which could stop the cons from using the mirror system. But sadly also stopped the officers from seeing the con in the cell, (due to how dark it was), when trying to do a roll check!! The lesser of two evils I suppose?

Georges Shop

Georges shop was the last stop on the bus to Fraggle City.

Every prison has workshops. It is in fact, a legal requirement that all adult male prisoners work. This comes in all forms, cooking and cleaning in the kitchens, cleaning on the wings, education classes and working in the workshops. Many of these were great places to learn a trade, such as bricklaying, plastering, carpentry, plumbing, welding, mechanics, in fact a very broad spectrum of courses designed to give the con a chance of employment after he is released. Alas most prisoners would see this as an unnecessary disruption to their sleeping, eating, smoking and gym sessions so there was seldom a certificate awarded.

Then there were the profit making workshops making things such as prison socks, t-shirts, jogging bottoms or plastic bowls, plates and cutlery. Outside contracts were also undertaken and provided a cheap way for manufacturers to produce goods such as lampshades, electrical fittings, clothing or repair of shopping trolleys.

Then there were the Fraggle shops. A Fraggle is a widely used term throughout the prison system for someone who is for whatever reason, inadequate. They cannot be trusted to work on the courses, as they are often not safe to use tools, either risking their own safety or that of others. They cannot be left to work on their own as usually their low I.Q's or volatile mental states would leave them in danger of injury, either by accident or self-inflicted. These guys were basically the bottom end of the prison food chain, and were always wide open to abuse from everyone. They needed to be cared for and nurtured, encouraged and supervised constantly. For this reason, coupled with the requirement to work, special shops need to be opened. The jobs were usually the most boring and sole destroying you or I could think of. But to the Fraggle it was very taxing or entertaining stuff that would keep them occupied for hours. Wonderfully rewarding work such as, sanding wooden coat hangers or packing little toys into plastic balls were the kind of things the poor inadequate's would find it hard to cope with. Incidentally, the old plastic ball fillers made the National papers one day, when mums up and down the country complained that unsuspecting kids were finding very rude and disgusting messages inside the balls. A shining example of the Fraggle mentality!

George was a mad Irish man with a mad reputation. Tall, white haired and wiry, he was an officer who had made it his mission to offer the unfortunates in his prison that little bit more. This was not your average Fraggle shop. Within reason, employees could do whatever they want. There was something for everyone, a bit of Chippying (Carpentry work), a bit of tailoring, various art based hobbies, making rocking horses for charity, or for many, just reading a newspaper or playing cards. As long as the Fraggle's turned up, they got paid. George would accept anyone, not just Fraggle's, as some lads enjoyed doing the charity stuff, which was sent to a local children's hospital ward. He did his best to encourage everyone who attended and with his abrupt and slightly eccentric ways, he got pretty good results. Some Frag's that hadn't spoke to staff for months let alone worked, produced some interesting stuff but best of all they were happy.

But the shop was not without problems. The mixture of Fraggle's and normal's often meant there was tension, as a fair amount of Fraggle baiting would take place. Well it was in the prisoner's unwritten book of rules. Thou must Fraggle Bait whenever possible or be forever deemed a wimp!

Jonesy was on shop patrol when he heard the bleep alert over his radio. This was the signal that an alarm bell had been pressed somewhere in the prison. It meant a member of staff was in danger or something bad was happening that required the help of any spare officers who could attend immediately. Jonesy, being on "shops" as it was known, was the first to swing into action, as the bell had been pressed in George's shop and he was just outside the back entrance. Problems were few and far between in George's shop, such was his control over the employees, so as Jonesy entered he feared the worst.

George was with Smithy. They both looked white, very white and were standing still in the middle of the large room which was full of deafening silence. The usually noisy, bustling shop was still and quiet as around 30 pairs of eyes homed in on Jonesy and then on to a solitary, short black lad at the opposite end of the shop, who was clutching a 10" pair of blood stained tailor scissors.

Jonesy had reached the scene very quickly and found himself alone and not sure what to do, obviously he needed to disarm the stabber and help the stabee, probably in that order, but self-preservation was kicking in and he was very loath to approach the stabber through fear of becoming the day's second victim!

"Go and get him Gov," someone shouted from somewhere in the silence.

"Yeah, go on Gov, he just stabbed Smithy." came a second shout.

A quick glance at Smithy revealed a number of red circles on his clothing. He looked a bit like a bad paintballer. Jonesy had to react. He ran at the stabber shouting, in the hope his display of balls would shock the stabber.

"DROP THE SCISSORS, DROP THEM NOW" and to his surprise he did just that. He dropped them to the floor and put his blood-covered hands in the air like he was starting a Mexican wave or had just been threatened by an armed bank robber. The stabber had his back to the door and fearing reprisals from the other cons, to the now unarmed man, Jonesy decided to bundle him out of the workshop door. Only about 30 seconds had elapsed since Jonesy's arrival at the shop and the cavalry had started to arrive too. As Jonesy was trying to push the stabber out, the staff were trying to come in. During the resulting mêlée, the cavalry assumed (luckily) that Jonesy was fighting the stabber, so grabbed the lad and marched him off to the Seg, trussed up like a Christmas Turkey.

The only weapon the staff have against violent prisoners is C&R, or Control and Restraint. This is a set series of well rehearsed moves, such as arm, wrist and leg locks, similar in style to that of many martial arts and are very effective in subduing a fighting prisoner. Today's stabber, although prepared to go quietly, felt the full force of the staffs C&R as they thought he had attacked Officer Jones who's shirt was now stained with the blood from the stabbers hands.

Jonesy's duties weren't finished yet though and he immediately ran back in to George and the leaky Smith to see what he could do? George was shouting random orders and starting to panic. Jonesy took over and sent George to direct the arriving staff to clear the innocent bystanders. Well I say innocent, but they were all guilty of something or they wouldn't have even been there……
He also shouted for an ambulance to be called. Smithy still said nothing. He was still standing on the same spot, in the same position as he was when Jonesy first arrived in the shop a full 3 minutes ago. He started to shake though as the shock kicked in and he didn't look good.
"Are you alright Smithy?" Jones chanced.
"Urgghhhh" was the only response.

Have you ever seen them cartoons like the roadrunner, or Tom and Jerry, where one of the characters is riddled with holes by a gun or a knife etc? Well this was the situation Jonesy now found himself in. On first inspection, Smithy didn't look too bad. Jonesy could only see one stab wound, noticeable by the hole in Smithy's shirt just above his left nipple. But as Jonesy watched the blood started to flow. Not just a trickle, more of a spurt. Jonesy immediately pushed the palm of his hand over the wound to stem the flow but it just squirted out between his fingers. As he did this he noticed another puncture wound in the top of Smithy's shoulder, just below his neck. This too started to squirt and Jonesy applied pressure to this hole with the other hand. Then another squirt appeared near the first. This was getting stupid and Jonesy called for help. Each time a hole was blocked, another was found. Quite a puddle was forming round their boots and the blood wasn't stopping. Taking the initiative, Jonesy slipped a finger inside the first hole in an attempt to stop the flow and it did the trick. So he slipped another finger into another hole, then another. His assistant did the same and before long, between them, they had seven wounds plugged with seven fingers. It looked like some macabre game of twister but the only colour was red. Various other wounds were present, but were mere trickles in comparison and it was deemed unnecessary to stick any other bodily parts into them at this stage. It was thankfully at this point, that the Paramedics turned up.

"Well you seem to have your hands full lads. Can you walk him to the Ambulance like that?"

So off went the officer / prisoner fusion to get treatment. Smithy looked like a human bowling ball. At the hospital Smithy's wounds were stitched up as one by one the officer's fingers were liberated from their warm and sticky positions. A couple of those deep wounds near the heart required surgery but Smithy made a full recovery. Unlike Jonesy's shirt, which was a write off.

So why did the Fraggle stab Smith?

"He was looking at me Governor!"

An Escape Fiasco

"All staff report to visits", is not something you often hear, or want to hear, especially after a long A Shift at 9 o'clock at night. So it was with much trepidation that the day staff filed into the visits hall this evening unsure of what the P.O. wanted from them.

Jonesy's usual jovial mood took a very quick dive as the staff were told that 3 prisoner's, (all Category "A"s, and 2 of which were lifers) had escaped during the evening from a nearby high security prison, and all those on duty had to go there immediately to assist in the search for the escapees.
Category "A" prisoners are those that are the highest risk in the prison system. They have usually committed the most violent or well-publicised crimes and would be a real embarrassment to the Home Office if they escaped, the fact that 2 of them were lifers was double trouble. These guys were always held in the most secure prisons and Jonesy knew that if they were still around it could be a very dangerous situation. This was not going to be a good night!

Like a herd of cattle the staff mooed and moaned as they wandered the short distance to their neighbouring prison, where they were let into a second visiting hall to receive a briefing from the duty Governor. Unfortunately he had heard about the escape earlier, so had pre empted his all night involvement and possible sacking for a botched job, by developing a very sudden illness and phoned in sick. So the job of I/C (In Charge) fell to the Security P.O. who had also heard about the escape and rushed in to help. All the staff knew and respected this man. They had all worked with him a lot and trusted him and his decision making. But under this immense pressure and in the heat of the moment, (he stood near the only working radiator in visits) the Guinea Pig, I mean man, made a few mistakes that all involved would regret later.

The next few minutes were crucial. Arrangements had to be made and contingency plans put into action. This would be a decisive time that could mean loss or re-capture of the escapees, (who turned out to be 3 very dangerous men indeed). One was in for plotting to kill the world with chemicals no less! So without further ado, plentiful supplies of tea bags and coffee were brought in from various private stashes accompanied by assorted biscuits. Also a couple of big portable boilers arrived to cope with the demand.

There was a lot of noise and even more commotion but nothing really seemed to be happening, except the obligatory tea and coffee consumption. Minutes slipped by and went into hours. Governors and P.O's came and went but no one addressed the staff and no one seemed to want to take charge of the situation, until the Security P.O. finally came in to tell the staff what he knew.

"Sometime during the evening, 3 Cat "A" prisoners have made good their escape. It is thought they left the wing at around 18:00 hrs with the rest of the prisoners going to the gym. It is then thought that they made their way to the metalwork shop, where they broke in and recovered tools and the pre-made parts of the ladder that now leans against the inside of the prison wall. From there, they cut through the various internal fences and the perimeter fence, carrying their pieces of ladder with them. They

then assembled the ladder and climbed the wall, further
making good their escape by shinning down a bedclothes
rope that was fastened to the top of the ladder.
 The next statement astounded Jonesy and it was at this
point he realised tonight was not going to go very well.

 "We would like you all to break up now into groups and
go round and search every building in the prison just to
make sure they have actually gone!"

 Jonesy thought to himself, but refrained from saying out
loud through fear of antagonising an already stressed
P.O.,
 "There are four fences with holes in them, a metal
workshop with half its tools missing, a ladder against the
outside wall that has been manufactured so well, you
could be forgiven for thinking the Fire Brigade had left it
there, attached to this is a finely crafted rope leading to
the safety of the road 25 feet below and you want us to
search to see if they have gone!? Did he really think they
would have gone to all that trouble just to have a picnic
on the sports field? Or maybe they had put all that
equipment there to cause a diversion, so they could go
and have a nice cup of tea with their mates on A Wing?
Was he bloody mad?"
 But search they did, for about a couple of hours in total.
Every building, wing, workshop and even the staff mess
(to get more supplies I would think) was looked into.
This did not go without incident either. The shops were
OK, although a little scary, as the thought that 3
desperate, crazed killers could jump out of the shadows
at any minute, was never far from the searchers minds.
But the wings threw up some major problems, as Jonesy

suspected, all the other prisoners were fully aware of the escape plan and were primed to deliver as many delay tactics to the staff as possible.

Each cell was opened, and each opener was met with a barrage of abuse. It was around 22:30 by now, so most of the cons were in their beds. Each volatile individual would leap up and start effing and blinding, questioning the staff's parentage and telling the staff to do something that involved copulation and travel. The staff were told, simply looking into each cell was not enough and they were told they had to look under the beds. Quite how they expected to find the three fugitives peeking out from under a bed, in a locked cell with only one entry point, that being the locked door they had just opened to enter, was beyond everyone. Most attempted entries resulted in a struggle or fight as each occupant threw himself in front of the bed as if to shield his 3 new pad mates. This kind of behaviour would normally have resulted in the prisoner's removal to the Seg unit but with more important things to do the staff turned a blind eye and all the cons got away with this outrageous behaviour.

So at around 23:00 ish it was finally agreed that the cons had actually climbed that ladder and left the establishment, making it time for the next stage of the operation.

There are strategic points around a prison that have to be manned at times like this. These are called fixed posts. There are maps with them clearly marked on but unfortunately these were not available. This particular prison had an inner and an outer ring due to its island location. Staff had to get to these posts and carry out continuous observations of the immediate area, reporting back any findings by radio. The outer posts were in strategic places such as Ferry Terminals or Marinas, (these had already been deployed). The inner posts were evenly spaced within a couple of miles or so from the prison, at main road junctions and some more secluded points. So the staff were split into three's and armed with a single radio, which may come in handy, to throw at the prisoners, if they are spotted later in the night. Unfortunately, the staff working in the communications room that night were new to the job and had little or no training between them. As staff tried to get through on their radios to join the net and receive a call sign, the ill-trained Comms room staff panicked with the sudden burden of their importance and shut down the system pretending it was broken. Or that's how it seemed, as absolutely no contact could be made, via radio, to the prison what so ever. Unperturbed the valiant and somewhat ill-prepared staff stepped out into the crisp winter air.

It was a very cold night in January. Frost and ice lay evenly over everything at ground level in the −9 degree night. Lots of lads who drove in that morning in their nice warm cars, or who got lifts in wearing only their shirts, now found themselves exposed to the elements and facing a freezing cold and potentially, very long night. No one had any idea how long they would be out for. It was now up to 5 hours since the 3 may have escaped and they could be a long way off the island by now, but the pre-set plans for this situation dictated the posts must be manned. So it was time for action. Jonesy and his 2 mates Dave and Anthony, had been given a post a good couple of miles from the prison. With no vehicle and only one coat between them, it was a very ugly prospect. The ice on the paths and roads was thick and dangerous in the dark and as they walked past a phone box a sudden thought struck Jones that could help them out. Little did they know that was the same phone box, one of the escaping cat "A"s used, to phone a taxi just a few hours before. Jonesy phoned his wife.

After a few preliminaries like "Where the fuck are you?" and "What the hell is going on?" from the Mrs. he soon found out that Dave and Anthony's wives were there too, as they had heard of the escape and being close friends had all got together thinking it would be safer. They all lived on the private Home Office built estate that housed many of the officers. Five minutes later Mrs. Jones turned up in the family car at the shivering officer's location, with an impressive array of ladies coats, these being the only ones available in abundance. She ferried the lads up to the point next to a huge dark forest, where they were to hold their late night vigil.

"Can I bring you anything else?" said Mrs. Jones with a distinct hint of worry in her voice.

"No", said Jonesy, trying to reduce her fear, "I doubt we'll be out long and I'm sure them bastards will be off the island by now. They probably had a boat waiting or something? You just go home, lock the doors, check the windows, shut the curtains and look after the kids. We'll see you when we finish."

Jonesy's house was on the edge of the forest on the opposite side to where he stood now. Secretly he feared the prisoners would be hiding up in the dense woodland and was worried his house may be a target, but did not let his wife know his concerns. He thanked her for the coats and sent her home with a kiss and a smile.

 So there they were. Three ruffty tuffty screws, dressed in a lime green silk jacket and a bright pink, ill-fitting fleece, armed only with a broken radio and a collective sense of humour, looking for three of the country's most desperate, hardened, on the run type criminals. Six rounds of I-Spy and a couple of Karaoke renditions later and the cold really started to penetrate. It was time to explore the surroundings. 50 yards up the road was an old wooden built, disused church hall. In American cop style formation, holding imaginary guns, they backed along the walls as if to sneak up on the prisoners round the next corner but found nothing. All they managed to do was scare each other by shouting as they jumped out round each corner. They stood by the wall, trying to shelter from the biting wind, and peered into the blackness between the trees, their gazes trying to penetrate deeper into the dense woodland. Every now and again one would see something moving and point it out to the others. For a few breathless seconds, they would all strain their eyes at the same point, but it always turned out to be the swaying of the trees or the rustling of some branches. My god, what would they do if these con's actually came out of the woods. Probably run a mile I should think at least to get help anyway.

 By now the cold, the freezing cold was really biting in as the time ticked past midnight and onto one o'clock. The spotter plane had been up for hours now and was continuously passing overhead, a sure sign that the police considered that the escapees could still be near. Every now and then a police car would whiz by, raising their excitement levels. The boys were in a remote area, so may not have seen as much action as others could have. It became necessary to jog around to try to keep warm. On the spot to start with, then up and down the road just a few yards at a time. Being competitive sorts, this quickly turned into a mini event, helping to warm the body and keep the boredom at bay. Then it was decided to pace out 100 yards up the hill to enable a 100-yard dash to the finish at the church hall. The race was on. Anthony being the fittest piped Jonesy at the post, but Jonesy claimed he had slipped on ice so demanded a rematch. It was now necessary to keep moving just to stay warm. So another sprint was held with Anthony winning this one hands down then the next and the next. Then Jonesy noticed the sound of distant sirens. The three jogged back to their post as the sirens got louder and the flash of blue lights started to light the night sky and illuminate the dark woods. All of a sudden the trees were ablaze with blue light as a speeding patrol car, not from the island but drafted in from the mainland just for the search, skidded to a halt on the ice right next to the sweaty prison officers. Jones, Dave and Anthony had already undone their coats.

1) To reduce their sweatiness.
2) To readily reveal their uniforms so as not to be confused with anyone undesirable.

It didn't work.

"What are you doing lads?" came the question from the policeman in the nice warm patrol car.

"Just out for a nice stroll, you Know!" came the sarcastic reply from Anthony.

"Shut the fuck up and answer the question", said the copper.

"Shut up, and answer? That might be a bit hard!" says Anthony, but copper was in no mood for games.

"What are you running around for?" says the copper getting impatient.

"We're keeping warm. Anyway, how did you know we were running around?" said an inquisitive and more co-operative Jonesy.

"Well you see that police spotter plane up there?" copper says as he points to the sky and the plane makes yet another well timed pass. "Well he keeps radioing our control room saying he spotted three men, possibly the escapees, running away from the scene, possibly trying to find a hiding place in the woods".

"Oh", comes a collective reply.

"So I'm gonna have to ask you lads to keep still".

"Bollocks!!" came another collective reply.

"Why on earth should we keep still? It's freezing!"

"Because I'm the one with the Heckler and Koch and I'm fucking telling you to!" says the irate copper.

The three faces slowly lowered their gaze to see the fully automatic weapon nestling snugly in the coppers lap, with an itchy finger hovering menacingly over the trigger. As they stared down they all agreed it would not be a good idea to piss this gun totting power junkie off any further and stood as still as possible.

It only then dawned on them how stupid the deployment of the officers had been. There was three prisoners missing and they send the staff out in threes. There must be little trios of prison officers all over the island, running round for warmth, confusing the shit out of the poor spotter plane crew.

Shortly after Arnold Swartzacopper left, a police van pulled up and asked the lads if they had seen anything. "Just one of your mob with a gun," snapped a pissed off Anthony. Then after a bit more dialogue, it was discovered that the police also had large numbers of officers out around the island (although not in threes) but they were doing half an hour on then half an hour off and had all been fed through the night by the local McDonalds. The poor prison officers had been out now for over 6 hours and hadn't even had contact with the prison, let alone had a break.

Anthony decided to try the radio again. After numerous presses of the button, switching on and off and shouting into it with no response, Anthony lost his temper and launched said useless radio high into the air on an arc that would certainly see its demise when it met the tarmac. As it reached the full height of its arc and started its landward journey, it sparked into life and the stressed and pensive voice was clearly heard to say, "This is control, go ahead officer Brown. Take call sign…….." but that was all they heard before their lifeline made contact with the frozen ground. It must have reached the required height needed to receive adequate signal strength from the distant prison. The battery skittered off one-way, the aerial bounced off another and the rest of the even more useless radio lay there in the ice, thirty yards up the race track, they used earlier in the night. Afraid to move through fear of attack by Helicopter Gunships, or a Napalm drop, the bemused officers stood in silence pondering their fate.

A bitterly cold hour or so later, a vision appeared, in the form of a prison van, driven by a couple of Auxiliaries from the lads own prison. Hoping to an end of their misery or at least a warm up in the van, a cup of tea and a break, they were elated. But the joy was short lived. The van had been tasked with driving round to see where all the prisons staff were and to drop off fresh batteries for the radios.

"Let us in the van" said Dave through chattering teeth.

"We can't" said the driver, "We gotta get round the whole island and report back."

"Well when you've done that, what about some hot drinks and food like the coppers?"

"Yeah OK, We'll do that." And with that they drove off and were never seen again.

The wee small hours were the worst. Huddled together and shivering like sheep on the moors, the three toughed it out until the sun's rays spread their warming arms over the tops of the houses on the hill they had used as their race track the night before, and engulfed them in its glow. Not one of them had a watch on, and they started to wonder what time the shop would open, also at the top of the hill. Enough was enough. This was an emergency. They were going to the shop to demand it opens so they could secure supplies for the troops. As they walked through the open door of the shop, (it had been open over an hour) they were greeted by an ecstatic little old lady, who was so pleased she had someone to tell about the great escape. It had been on the telly all night, blah blah blah. She was even more excited to talk to three men who had been involved in the whole sorry affair. She quizzed the lads while plying them with much needed hot drinks and free food from the shop, which was a good job, as they didn't have a penny between them and not enough strength to mug the old granny for her wares.

At about 11:30am, back at the fixed post, the lads were told the search was off, by a passing cop car and so made the long walk back.

It was almost a week later that one of the officers who had actually been suspended over the escape, (he was on duty on the wing the night they got out) spotted all three of the escapees walking along a road not 4 or 5 miles from the prison. He instantly informed the police and after a futile chase, where the chemical killer tried to make a run for it, by swimming the local river, (so I suppose he made a swim for it?) all three were back in custody.

Shortly after that, the actual details of what the escapees actually did that night were released.

They had left the wing that night to go to the gym, although none of them ever really used it. The other cons also leaving at that time had been primed and helped the 3 by trying to confuse and disrupt the staff that was counting them off the wing. Usually this wing only had a handful of cons that used the gym facilities but that night there was about 40 or 50 trying to make their way off the wing. Once off, certain selected individuals would turn and come straight back on, saying they had changed their minds or forgot their kit. Eventually the staff didn't have a clue how many had gone and relied on the gym staff to count them all in once they reached their destination. On the way to the gym though, which involved walking outside across various yards, the 3 snuck off into the shadows and were not missed when the staff counted them in at the end of their journey. When the gym session was finished, the same number as were counted into the gym, were returned back, so the 3 were not detected as missing until the night time roll check at around 20:00hrs. This gave them enough time to execute their plans.

During this time they did indeed break into the Metal Workshop, where they had been working for some months prior to this event. Due to the lack of security consciousness and commitment on behalf of the shop instructors, they were able to make and secrete around the workshop, various pieces of a clip together ladder. This night they retrieved the ladder pieces and some tools to cut the fences. This prison, although housing Cat "A" prisoners had no Geophone system in place. This is an electronic system that detects any unusual movement on the fences and sounds an audible alarm in the Comms room when activated, so it was an easy route to the outside wall. Once in the sterile area, the area between the outer fence and the wall, a kind of no man's land, they assembled the ladder and attached the homemade rope to the top so they could lower themselves down the other side. When they hit the street, they went straight into the public payphone box on the corner of the wall and called a taxi, probably using money that had been smuggled in earlier. I can't imagine the following dialogue would have taken place during a reverse charge call!

"Hello, I have a homicidal axe wielding maniac on the line, will you accept the charges?"

"Of course put him through!"

"Listen. I killed loads of people right, and I'm with two mates that done the same. We just broke out the slammer yeah, and we want a car to the local airfield so we can nick a plane and fuck off abroad."
"Certainly sir, ten minutes OK?"

Anyway, the taxi turned up and noticed nothing untoward, as the cons in this prison were allowed to wear their own clothes. No arrowed uniforms or anything recognisable here. They were dropped at their destination, the local airfield, where they purchased tools from the local petrol garage, and proceeded to try to steal a plane. One of the 3 was a trained pilot!
Now forgive me if I sound a bit defeatist, or am I missing something here. Their on an Island, surrounded by water, wouldn't it have just been a tad easier to steal a boat!? I mean a plane is just a bit harder to steal surely? And what if they crashed it? That's death in my book. You crash a boat you can swim to safety! Well thanks to the determination of the owner of the plane and his desire to keep his aircraft firmly on the ground unless he was in it, he had disabled it sufficiently enough to scupper the guys hijacking attempts. Phew…………..
Good grief, thinking about it, the Island was only about a mile from the coast off the mainland, they could have bloody swam across in 30 minutes. Mind you they would have had to negotiate the busiest shipping lane in the world, and dealt with the minus 9 temperatures but even that was a better chance than nicking a non-flyable plane.
So, having spent a week hiding in some shed or god knows where, there they were walking along the side of

the road, just asking to be recaptured. They might as well have knocked back on the door of the prison they escaped from. The management probably wouldn't have noticed!

Diamond Minder

The Diamond Minder was as mad as they come. He was only on the wing about 6 months but caused more incidents in that time than the rest of the residents put together.

"I'll be going home soon. I'm innocent. So there's no point in telling me all the bollocks about the wing or trying to put me on any courses", Smith said on his first day on "C" Wing. He was as fit a man as Officer Jones had ever seen. Scarily so! This guy had muscles on his muscles and his veins stood out like the gnarled roots of an ancient oak. He was in his late 20's but was as wise as the Dali Lama. He was black with the small twisty dreads of a would be Rasta. His glasses hid wild eyes and the overall studious look hid the madness that had caused him to move from prison to prison to prison. He was incredibly powerful with amazing stamina. This made him very hard to control. He had no problems with prison staff, after all, as far as he was concerned, he was innocent but he hated the system. He found it hard to follow orders and this had caused various conflicts since his first imprisonment. Staff that would normally walk all over a subversive prisoner, struggled to hold Smith in any kind of restraining lock, such was his power. He could ignore pain and fight any amount of men at the same time. He found himself in this particular prison as they were experts in dealing with his kind.

After a week or so of settling in, Smithy was finding his

feet. He was becoming confident and started to display the kind of behaviour that had worried staff in the previous establishments he had wrecked.

The first party piece he decided to show off was his chair trick. Smith was a martial arts expert and had incredible balance. Just outside the wing office he appeared with two plastic chairs. The kind you would find in any place with, plastic chairs. He stood them back to back about 6 inches apart on the well polished lino floor. He then stood facing the chairs beyond which was the open office door. The officers inside the office, although busy, had noticed Smith just outside the door, standing with eyes closed, breathing deeply with two plastic chairs.

Suddenly he jumped into the air and landed with his two bare feet onto the thin backs of the chairs, one foot on each. Now he suddenly had the staff's full attention! With his eyes still closed he very slowly started to slide the chairs apart, showing amazing strength and control until he was in the splits position on top of the backs of the chairs.

"What the hell is he doing?" said one of the bemused officers.

"Fuck knows!" said another.

He then started to bounce, to the point where his crutch was almost touching the floor, while his feet still gripped the backs of the motionless chairs. Then in an even more amazing display of strength and balance, he managed to draw the chairs back together again until he was standing back upright on the tops of the chairs which were now back in their original positions. Smith jumped one more time but this time a backward somersault saw him land softly back behind the chairs. He picked them up and walked off without a word to the amazed staff. He hardly broke a sweat. The staff had seen nothing like it. They were suddenly in awe of this man's incredible power and knew that this amazing display was to warn them, mess with me and you'll come unstuck!

The second party piece Smith had up his sleeve was his ability to dislocate his thumbs. No one really knew why he did this but it was impressive never the less. He could bend those suckers into all kinds of strange angles. Possibly it was the years of accidents and abuse to the joints that had caused it but it did enable him to do one very worrying thing. He could slip handcuffs with ease. This, in a prison environment, was a huge problem. Whenever a prisoner was taken anywhere outside of the prison he had to be handcuffed, either to another prisoner or to an officer. The escorting officer had to ensure the cuffs were applied correctly. This means above the wrist bone and tight enough to stop them slipping down to the hand but not so tight as to stop the blood flow. It was quite an art to get it right.

The first time staff found out Smith could do this was not on an escort but while they were trying to escort him to the segregation unit. Another prisoner had foolishly tried to steal something from his cell Smith had of course dealt out some swift and well deserved punishment and while the victim was on his way to hospital to be patched up, Smith was on his way to the Seg. When a prisoner is compliant, he can be walked to the Seg peacefully. It is usually recommended though that cuffs are applied to prevent any further shenanigans. Tempers can flare straight after an incident with the adrenaline flowing, so it's considered safer for all involved to cuff the attacker. Although Smith was compliant on this occasion, as far as he was concerned, he had done nothing wrong. Why should he go anywhere? All he did was sort out the wing thief! He did the staff a favour. Fearing a fight, the P.O. in charge, applied the cuffs to Smiths wrists and ordered the staff to walk him down. No more than two steps later, Smithy handed the cuffs back to the P.O.

"Shit! I must have not locked them properly" he said with surprise.

He put them back on, tighter this time and two steps later found himself holding them again.

"Smith, what the fuck are you doing? How did you do that?" said the angry P.O.

He had been made to look foolish. He applied the cuffs once more but this time got two burly officers to apply wrist locks to stop him slipping out again. Ten seconds later the cuffs were flying towards the P.O. and the officers were flying towards the floor. That was it, game on! The assembled staff jumped on Smith and one by one they were thrown off. Eventually the sheer weight of numbers got him to the ground and some very experienced officers were attempting to put wrist locks on Smith. Unfortunately, many of the wrist locks involved holding the thumbs in some way and of course that wasn't going to work with Smithy. Every time they bent his wrists he just straightened them. Some of these guys actually taught C&R (control and restraint) techniques to the other staff and they just couldn't seem to get a lock on. There was no noise! Usually during a bend up, as a C&R take out was known, the poor recipient of the locks would be squealing with pain as these locks are designed to hurt so that the person being restrained complies with the officers' instructions. But Smithy didn't utter a sound. He simply closed his eyes and went into a trance like state, completely resisting and ignoring the sweaty officers' efforts. Eventually Smith said,

"Look. Just tell me what you want me to do?"

"We want you to go to the Seg" shouted one of the sweaty officers.

"Then get the fuck off me and I'll walk down there" said Smith calmly.

The assembled staff were very loath to do this expecting him to go mad when he was released but had very little choice. Once any trouble had gone this far, the only way to the Seg was under full restraints but due to Smithy's power and thumb based magical powers, it was proving impossible. So he was walked and true to his word he caused no further trouble and was fully compliant.

His behaviour in the Seg was impeccable over the next few days and eventually it was decided to try him back on the wing. It was at this stage that Officer Jones decided to try to get to know Smithy a bit better, rather having him as an ally than an enemy. Jonesy wanted to find out more about him and his past. Why did he think he was innocent? Why was he so sure he would soon be released?

Mr. Goldberg was a Diamond Dealer and a very successful and wealthy man. As he walked through the doors of a very well known Knightsbridge store he was confident, happy and looking forward to clinching a long awaited sale. As he strode through the various departments he didn't notice the suited Asian man who was tailing him from a distance. Two more Asians were closing in from another angle and suddenly the robbery was on. All three Asians attacked the Diamond dealer with a vicious ferocity. Grabbing the small brief case from the dealers hand the leader of the gang screamed abuse as he realized the case was handcuffed to the owner's wrist. The bright store lights glinted off the huge blade as it was lifted by the leader. The brightness momentarily blinded the dealer and in a flash the blade came down and plunged up to the handle into the heart of its victim. As he fell, a fourth man arrived on the scene and went to work. The muscular black man threw a bone crunching punch at the knife wielding attacker, smashing his jaw and sending teeth flying. He grabbed the hand that held the knife and in one smooth fast movement snapped the arm and threw the blade across the shop. The second attacker rushed to assist his accomplice. As he came in the black man aimed a kick at the man's throat. The Asian reeled back in agony hardly breathing and made a hasty retreat as he gagged and vomited from the blow. The third man picked up the first and they ran for their lives. They had not bargained on the dealer's minder being there.

Smith the minder had been shadowing his boss and was a bit too far away when the attack took place. He was mortified that he had let his boss down and was now desperately trying to revive him and stem the blood loss. As he leant over his boss with his hands firmly pressed on the large wound in his chest, he almost blacked out as he felt a skull crushing blow across the back of his head. With claret pumping from the split in his scalp he turned to see a new assailant standing over him with a truncheon in his hand. As the second blow arced through the air, Smithy aimed a punch at the attackers Solar Plexus. Fearing this was another gang member he quickly removed the man's weapon by snapping his arm and decked him with another blow to his jaw. Security guards rained down from everywhere to subdue the black man with blood on his hands.

 Officer Jones and Smithy had built up quite a relationship over the last few weeks. They had a mutual respect for each other due to their love of martial arts. So when it was announced that Smith was to be admitted to hospital to have his weakened thumbs pinned, Jonesy was the natural choice to escort him.
 Smith had confided in him all the details of his case. He had been arrested for the attempted murder of a Mr. Goldberg, a rich Diamond dealer and a serious case of GBH on a Police officer, who had found Smith leaning over the stabbed man. The officer was attacked by Smith after trying to subdue him with his truncheon as he thought he had stabbed the man on the floor.
 Smith's boss was still alive though and since the attack had been lying in a coma and was in a bad way. In the absence of any other attackers and with no other witnesses coming forward, the police officers word was taken and Smithy found himself doing an 8 year sentence for attacking the man he was actually trying to save.

 As he lay in the prep room, waiting for his own operation, Smithy told Officer Jones he was a good man, then handed him the cuffs that were supposed to be on his wrists to stop him escaping.
 "Will you pack that up?" said Jonesy as he put the cuffs back on for the third time and wondered if it was worth it as he would only do it again.
"Hello Mr. Smith, I'm the Anaesthetist" said the Anaesthetist, "I'm just going to put you to sleep."
"That sleepy juice won't work on me man! I'm not going

to sleep", said a defiant Smithy.

The Anaesthetist injected the large syringe of milk like fluid into Smiths hand and waited for the desired effect. But nothing happened.

"That sleepy juice ain't gonna work man", smiled Smithy again.

"This is irregular. I'll give him another one", said the Anaesthetist and he did give him another one just like he said he would, then waited.

"I ain't gonna go sleep", chirped Smith.

"He bloody is!" said the Anaesthetist "I'll give him another one!" and he did. He told the staff at this point that the sleepy juice to weight ratio was enough to knock out an Elephant and he had never needed to use so much. "I ain't no Heleflant an I ain't gonna go sweep!" said a drowsy Smith. Half way through the fourth syringe he finally went out. The Anaesthetist was worried he killed him. As he lay there drifting off, he slipped the cuffs again and Jonesy knew he would be ok. An hour or so later his thumbs had been pinned and he was wheeled through to recovery. Jonesy put the cuffs on, happier that they would stay on this time, now that his thumbs were fixed. But within only a few minutes and before Smithy had fully awoken, there were two stomach churning cracks as Smithy dislocated both thumbs and snapped the Titanium pins, subsequently slipping the cuffs again!

"What a waste of time that was", said Jonesy "We better wake him up and get him back to the nick", and they did. Within a day or two Smith had delved into the wounds and removed the pins with his bare hands and refused any further treatment.

He patiently waited for any news of his boss and looked

forward to going home soon. A few weeks later the call came. Mr. Goldberg had woken from his Coma.

Although obviously confused and disorientated the first thing he asked was where was his minder? The police at his bedside asked what he meant. He said,

"Paul Smith, my minder, he saved my life. He chased off the men who attacked me and gave me first aid. Where is he?"

"Erm…………..He's doing 8 years for your attempted murder!"

So a witness was finally found. What better witness than the man who saw it all, the man who was attacked? Smithy was elated. He knew he would get out and was back by his boss's side within days of his release.

How to Get to the Block in One Easy Lesson!

There are many reasons that cons want to go to the block. The Prison Segregation Unit or Block as it is known is primarily an area of the prison that is used for punishments. It is where all the adjudications are held. Any misdemeanours or offences against prison rules will result in adjudication a kind of mini court case chaired by the Governor of the prison. The cons see these as Kangaroo courts and usually claim to be not guilty even if they know they are banged to rights. To the staff this is one of the only ways to get their own back against some of the con's appalling behaviour.

The block can also be used to house those that seek protection from other prisoners, drug dealers that have been removed from their wing and are awaiting transfer, or to house those too difficult to be dealt with in a normal wing environment. Dangerous individuals who would fight officers at the drop of a hat were put on "Lie Downs." They could be moved from Block to Block up and down the country for perhaps a month at a time, constantly unsettling them, but giving each block a well earned rest.

So as you can see, there are many customers and there is no room for anyone who doesn't need to be or shouldn't be there. A major problem in many prisons though was prisoners trying to go down there as and when they wanted. More often than not someone would get in debt on the wing and want to run for cover. Another may get a knock back on a parole hearing or home leave application and suddenly want out the place. They may just get the hump with someone or something and get a big sulk on, behave like a child and want to go to the Block while stamping their feet in a big strop. Of course it comes down to the officers to calm them down and convince them they are better off staying where they are on the wing.

But when a con was adamant (I don't mean Stuart Goddard, that stripe face freak from the 80's) I mean when they were determined, there was not much you could do to stop them. The Officers are the link from Wing to Block and usually the only way a con was going down there is if the alarm bell had been pressed by an officer for assistance during an incident. Each Prison has an alarm bell system with buttons strategically placed, so that if there is any trouble anywhere around the prison, someone can press the bell linked to a central control room, this is then broadcast over the radios net and any spare staff will hear the call and attend the area to assist the officer in trouble.

Smith came to the office and uttered the immortal words, "I wanna go to the Block!"

"Yeah whatever Smithy off you go" said an uninterested officer Jones.

"I wanna go to the Block!!" Smith said louder and more agitated than the first.

"You can't! Now clear off!" replied a more agitated Officer Jones

"Look, I ain't Fucking about. I want off this wing right now so take me down the Block you prick."

"There's no need to start getting nasty. Don't start swearing. You know you can't just go down the Block as when you want. What's the problem?" said Jonesy.

"It's nothing to do with you. What have I got to do? Just get me down the Block!"

There was obviously going to be no reasoning with this guy but Officer Jones managed to usher Smith away from the office.

Ten minutes later he was back. More pissed off and more eager to get off the wing.

"Gov I want to get off the wing, take me down the Block!"

"Look Smith I already told you", advised Jonesy, "You can't go down the Block for no reason."

"What do I have to do?" questioned Smithy.

"All sorts of things will work Smithy", said Officer Jones trying to inject a bit of humour into a volatile situation.

"Oh there's various things you could do mate. Refuse to bang up. Have a fight with another con, that's always a good one. If your desperate, assault a member of staff, that's a sure fire way of a one way ticket. Damage prison property! Sticking a chair through the office window would work!"

Jonesy thought there was enough there for the irate loon to think about.

Smithy skulked off again to consider his options.

Five minutes later and without warning the safety glass in the office window splintered into a thousand flying shards and showered the assembled staff within the office. Obviously the final option had struck a chord with Smithy and he brought the metal framed chair down with such ferocity that it wedged into the wire mesh contained within the glass and stuck there for all to see.

The officers didn't need to be asked again and while a slightly shaken, glass covered Jonesy pressed the bell, and a smug looking Smith was removed to where he wanted to be.

Smithy's little plan didn't stop there though. He had another trick up his sleeve that may save him from further trouble.

The following morning the adjudication was held. Officer Jones had nicked Smith for damaging Prison property. The Governor read out the charge and asked Smith why he had smashed the window.

Calmly and with not a hint of a smile he said, "Coz Officer Jones told me to!"

"Is this true Officer Jones?" said the Governor as he turned his gaze onto the squirming Officer.

"Well not exactly!!" claimed Jonesy....................

Passport Control

Every now and again an opportunity comes up that you just don't want to miss. Imagine being given the chance of an all expenses paid trip to some far off shores, with the added bonus of stocking up on some duty frees. Who could turn that down?

A con on "A" Wing was originally from Jersey. All his family still lived there, so he hadn't seen them since his conviction a year or so before. After six month's a prisoner becomes eligible to be temporarily transferred to a local prison close to their home address, for accumulated visits. All the unused visiting orders would be saved up and then used over a 4-week period, to see all their family in one go.

In order for this to take place, arrangements must be made to transfer him to the local prison where the visits will take place and then be bought back again. These days all the escorts are done by private security firms, but years ago it was down to the officers of the holding prison to take him there and bring him back.

So it was with much excitement that officer Jones anticipated the chance to take Smith home to Jersey for his visits. One of Jonesy's colleagues from his wing, did all the groundwork and contacted HMP Le Moye, the only prison in that area, and arranged the transfer. Each prisoner has an officer assigned to him to do all his paper work and sort out any problems he has. This is known as the Personal Officer. Although Jonesy was not Smith's personal officer he hoped that there may be some way he could get involved in the upcoming trip.

Then a few days prior to the trip, he noticed two officers names on the detail board showing who would be lucky enough to be escorting Smith home……………it wasn't Jonesy!

"Damn it", he thought and straight away started planning a scam.

The next day, (the day before the escort), Jonesy went to find officer Young, one of the staff with the golden ticket. He had little experience in the job and was deemed the more likely of the two to fall for his little plan.

"Looking forward to your little trip then?" Jonesy dropped into the conversation he had started with Young ten minutes ago.

"Yes", said Young, "should be a good'un. Never been to Jersey before."

"Really", said a devious Jonesy working his magic. "Your passport up to date?"

"Shit", says Young. "I haven't got one. Do you need a passport for Jersey?" he said in panic.

"Yeah or course you do. It's just off the French coast ain't it?" said Jonesy while trying to suppress his smug smile.

"Shit" said Young again, "I ain't got a passport and there is no time to get a visitor one today, I'm on an "A" shift"

These "A" shifts were particularly nasty, 07:30 until 21:00. It gave you no time to do anything in a day except work.

"You told the detail office you would do the escort though mate?" quizzed Jones.

"Yeah, course I have. Shit", Young was gutted but worried he would get in trouble for letting the detail staff down so close to the escort.

"Hey look. I've got a passport. Why don't I nip up the

detail office for you and tell them that something has come up and you can't make it. I'm a rest day and don't mind going instead. I had something else planned, but I don't mind cancelling it, you know, to help out a mate"

"Would you do that mate? Thanks a lot. I'd really appreciate it."

"Tell you what, do you want me to bring you back some smokes or a bottle? You must be disappointed?

"No don't worry mate. I'm just glad you've got me out the shit with the detail." said a very worried Young.

A few days later after a very successful trip, Jonesy had to make himself scarce, as a well-miffed Mr Young was on the warpath. The other lads had got wind of Jonesy's game and had made a passport control sign and stuck it over the entrance to Young's wing. Thankfully he saw the funny side and Jonesy lived again.

*Incidentally. Talking of Jersey. There was a dirty old man on the wing around the same time, who among other things, had been arrested for having sex with a cow. The officers took great pleasure in saying to him, whenever the temperature dropped,

"Cor it's Friesian in here, why don't you slip into a Jersey?" Boom Boom.*

Seg Tennis

Smith was one of the most notorious prisoners in the system. His antics were always well documented in the national papers and he himself has written a few books on his exploits during his stay at Her Majesty's Pleasure. To say he was a handful was an understatement. He was so volatile he had spent most of his time in Segregation, being moved from Seg unit to Seg unit, up and down the country. There are plenty of staff from high security establishments with stories about Smith "On the Roundabout." This is a term used to describe how a dangerous or highly disruptive prisoner is sent from prison to prison, usually Seg to Seg, mainly to give the various prisons used, and their staff, a break from the constant attention these men would require. "On a lie down" is another term used, which comes from the constant lock up and 23hrs a day these men would lie on their beds, in their cells. It is hardly surprising they would come out fighting, having been driven mad from all the messing about. Mind you most of them were as mad as a box of frogs well before finding their way into their first Seg unit.

Depending on the category of the prison, the Seg staffing could be anything from an S.O. and 3, (meaning one senior officer and three officers) up to an S.O. and 8 or 10 or more. Some prisons, like category "D" don't even have a Seg as the prisoners are very low risk. Top security prison Segs can hold many prisoners and are very busy. There is little time to deal with problems as many jobs need to be done to complete the daily routine.

Each prisoner is entitled to one hour of exercise per day. With two small exercise yards to use and only about 6 useable hours per day, it don't take much to work out the difficulties faced in exercising 20 to 30 men. This added to the showers, phone calls, applications and feeding, the days are busy and any disruptions are a pain in the arse.

Smith was a fierce mountain of a man. Incredibly fit and strong and an ex-prize fighter, he would take on any man or men. But he had and incredibly volatile temper and an extreme dislike for authority. His life in prison was never going to be a bed of roses. Incidents were regular. Injuries to staff were common place and he stretched the prisons resources to its limits.

"Alarm bell Seg unit," came across the radio in its usual urgent sounding manner. The response team, housed in an office in the centre of the prison immediately jumped into action. Any alarm bell is treated as urgent. Sometimes the alarm was real, sometimes false, but each was treated as if staff were in danger. An alarm bell in the Seg though, usually meant there was a major problem. This particular prison was lucky enough to have spare staff, who would be on standby to attend to any trouble spots. On this occasion there were about 12 or 15 so they were collectively confident they could deal with whatever they found. As the gate and the door to the Seg swung open, the confidence of many of them quickly drained as they saw Smith standing over 3 unconscious staff, holding a table leg in each hand, shouting, "who's next?"

Obviously the serving of today's meal had not gone as

smoothly as the unconscious staff on the floor would have liked! Smith's beans had probably been too hard or he didn't get enough black bits in his peas, or something else equally as important. So he had smashed the table, redecorated the walls with the day's food and knocked out any staff that were stupid enough to step into the arc of the flailing busted table legs. You could hear the collective, screeching skid of rubber soles on highly polished floor as the cavalry came to a rapid stop, when their self preservation mechanisms naturally kicked in. Those at the front were edging back and those at the back were pushing forward, no one wanting to be the first to engage the enemy or at least the swinging table legs. Thankfully, someone had remembered to grab a riot shield on their way to the fray and it was passed over the top of the group to the front man. Officer Jones now found himself holding this shield. Probably the lightest man there, he had found himself at the front due to his endless marathon training. Not wanting to look scared in front of his pals, though he clearly was, he let out a war cry, (which came out "Oh bollocks I'm dead") and started to run at Smith protected by the shield. The rest of the group, not expecting Jonesy to be quite so Gung Ho, were taken by surprise and took up the charge about 5 paces behind. The noise of wood on poly-carbonate shield was disturbing enough but the speed at which skinny Jonesy and the shield flew through the air, was much more worrying for the people behind, as the pieces of wood were now swinging in their direction. Two more staff hit the deck with serious facial injury, before the sheer weight of numbers took Smith to the floor amid the water, potatoes, veg and laser cut wafer thin beef, that had long since flew through the air before them.

Smithy wasn't finished though. He was very powerful in the arms, shoulders and chest and proceed to throw 18 stone men off him like rag dolls. As each one flew another one took his place. One by one they were dispensed and one by one they jumped back on. Jonesy, now back on his feet, wanted more action. Buoyed up by the fact he had survived his first assault and the fact that Smith was on his back, he rejoined the mêlée on the top of the heap of bodies. Then a well aimed loose arm, connected an even better aimed loose fist with Jonesy's jaw and his involvement in the removal of Smith to the special cell ended as quickly as it started.

This kind of behaviour was usually a massive hindrance to the smooth running of the Seg but the staff managed to use it to their advantage on this occasion.

Smith was very vocal. All the other prisoners were very aware of his presence. He was like a prisoner hero and they all took great delight in goading and encouraging him from behind their doors, every time he kicked off with the staff. But Smith's frustration and anger was not only vented at staff. Anyone who dared upset him, would risk serious assault.

One of Smith's favourite things was to exercise on the yard with a medicine ball. Have you felt the weight of one of them bloody things? For his whole hour of exercise, he would lie on his shirtless back, on the crumbling tarmac floor, and throw the medicine ball into the air and catch it on his stomach. When I say throw it in the air, I mean launch it like a trebuchet to a height exceeding 20 feet and each time it would land on his stomach. At the end of this relentlessly sweaty hour, he would be led back to his cell, hardly breathing, already looking forward to his next session.

On this particular bright sunny day exercise was very popular. Smith was in yard 1 doing his usual and some insignificant guy was in yard 2. The yards were basically two fenced in cages about 40 feet x 40 feet with 20 foot fencing all around an 18 foot high bare breeze block wall dividing the two areas, so the occupants could not see each other or easily converse.

I'm not sure whether the sun was in Smithy's eyes or something but for the first time, the medicine ball, having been launched on an adverse angle, found its way over the top of the dividing wall into the opposite yard.

"Throw that back over?" Smith shouted as if it was the most normal and manageable thing for any man to do. The yard 2 con, looked at the ball, realised it was the legendary Smith on the other side of the wall and thanked god his identity was hidden by the barrier. He swallowed deeply and did his best to lift the ball off the floor and at this point it became blatantly obvious he would not manage the super human feets that his opponent was expecting of him. But as the encouragement and abuse came through the wall, adrenaline and probably the fear of a long slow death, kicked in and yard 2 con surprised himself and the assembled staff by getting the missile over in a one er.

Seg Tennis was born!!

Smith was chuffed to bits with this new found distraction and wanted more. He swiftly huzzed the ball back over the wall and waited expectantly for a quick return. The look of horror on yard 2 cons face as the ball returned to his feet, was a joy to the assembled staff. A few nods in

the direction of yard 1 from the beaming staff was all
yard 2 con needed to ask to finish his exercise. Smith
exploded.

"You'd better get that ball back over that wall or I will rip
your head off and shit down your neck!" Smith said as
well as other words of encouragement. Yard 2 con
panicked and pleaded to be escorted back to his cell but it
was game on. No on stepped forward to release the poor
victim from his hell. They wanted to see what developed.
Fuelled by pure fear and to the staff's amazement the ball
flew back over. Bets were quickly taken as to how many
more times he could do it. Again Smith launched it over
at such high velocity it bounced off the back fence. Yard
2 con managed one more return and then it was game, set
and match to Smith as yard 2 con collapsed in a sweaty
heap. As the staff led the loser back to his cell, Smith was
like a Tasmanian devil bouncing off the fence on his side
of the yard. He had caught a glimpse of his unworthy
opponent and spent the next ten minutes telling him what
he was going to do with his gizzards, his father's gizzards
and various entrails of his mother, sister and basically all
friends and family. The C&R team arrived and dragged
Smith off to his second home, the box.

Next day, Smith had calmed down and was in the yard
looking for a new opponent. News of Seg Tennis had
gone round and a few fool hardy tough nuts thought they
could rise to the challenge. One by one they were led out
for 3 or 4 throws each, before they were led back past the
usual threats about gizzards, death, families, deaths of
families etc. Even the most hardened and fittest of the
Seg occupants could not keep up with Smith's relentless
stamina and power. Smith's frustration and rage

overflowed and a few more days were spent in the box.

 On his next visit to the yard an amazing thing happened. Smith was safely contained within yard 2, which meant that any possible opponent would have to be walked past him so he would see who they were. The staff walked round the cells, as they had done for years, offering the morning exercise, and the response was the same from every single door.

"Exercise?" said the staff.

"Is Smithy on the yard?"

"Yep."

"Then no, I won't bother."

The next door.

"Exercise?"

"Is Smith on the yard?"

"Yep!"

"NO!"

Next door.

"Exercise?"

"Is that Smith on the yard?"

"Oh yes!"

"Fuck that!"

It was a revelation, never before had there been so many refusals. Sometimes if the weather was shite, a few wouldn't bother but for many Seg dwellers, this was the only escape from the confines of their pokey little cell and was seldom missed.

 The next day, the staff put Smith out first into yard 2 and the same thing happened.

"Exercise?"

"Is Smith on the yard?"

"Yep"

"Bollocks!"

All the way round the cells. The staff were chuffed to bits. With so many refusals, their work load was practically halved. The two staff that had to monitor the yards could be re-deployed to other more important tasks within the unit, like making tea and toast. For the first time in years the Seg staff had spare time on their hands and were loving it.

Even in the afternoon session, they told the cons that Smith was out on the yard, even though he had his hour in the morning, and true to form, they all declined. No one wanted to risk the wrath of Smith!

Eventually Smith was shipped out to another prison. But for some THREE months after he had gone, the Seg staff enjoyed easier days with no exercise. Every time exercise was offered, each con was told that Smith was on the yard and even though no one had seen or heard him for weeks, the fear the man left in their hearts was too great to contemplate venturing out.

Silence in Court

The Old Bailey was a formidable but impressive place.
The decor as well as the attitudes was stuck in the dark
ages. Although clean, the whole place looked like it was
coated in 100's of years of grime. The court rooms
themselves were dark and foreboding, lined with old oak
panelling. Seated on oak benches it was hardly the most
comfortable of places to be during long drawn out cases.
There was a musty smell and with very little natural light
and was the least favourite job of many a weary escorting
Prison Officer.

Jonesy was on duty with a particularly old but very wise
S.O. They had been tasked with producing one of their
prisoners at the court for further sentencing. It was a very
hot day and the case was extremely boring. It wasn't long
before the S.O. started to nod off. Jonesy did what he
could to keep the S.O. awake. The bemused con was
sitting between the two officers and was happy, to start
with, in assisting Jonesy to stop the S.O. sleeping. Every
now and again he would kick the S.O's foot when Jonesy
instructed him to do so.

Then the snoring started. Quiet at first but then the deep
rumbles started to reverberate around the huge court
room. The Judge started to twitch and fidget and tried to
spot where the noise was coming from. High court
Judges are not to be messed with! They are very
respected people with amazing powers. Not only could
they have anyone held in contempt of court for disturbing
his proceedings, which in itself could lead to prosecution,
they could also turn a man to stone (I had heard) with one
look of a beady eye!!

Jonesy was worried! The S.O. was 30 years his senior in experience and he didn't want to see him in trouble. There was also an unwritten rule that junior staff, give long serving experienced staff the utmost respect at all times. The old dinosaurs must never be questioned and any decisions they made or orders they gave must be strictly adhered to. Jonesy was in a quandary, he didn't want to disturb his colleague but definitely didn't want to see him in trouble as he knew it would be his fault. So he asked the con to give him a nudge but by now the prisoner was tired of all the messing about. After all he was trying to hear what was decided about his future and refused to help.

The snoring was getting louder and the Judge was getting more restless. Jonesy was really worried for his colleague.

Then BOOM! The S.O's head snapped back and smashed against the hollow wooden panelling behind his seat. The sound echoed round the room like a gunshot making all assembled jump then fall silent as the Judge jumped to his feet.

Within a millisecond of his head hitting the panelling the S.O. leapt to his feet and threw a perfectly aimed hand in the direction of Jonesy's blushing cheek. It slapped him hard and as it connected the S.O. shouted,

"Sorry your honour! It's the boys first time in court. I'm sorry he's messing about. I'll sort him out later. Carry on!"

Jonesy had tears in his eyes and the con almost pissed himself laughing.

So much for staff loyalty....................

Sausages

Sooner or later a prisoner is going to fall out with an officer. It is inevitable. In prison as in normal life, you meet a whole host of different characters. People from all walks of life find themselves on the wrong side of a judge. At the same time, there are loads of different officers with loads of different personalities and backgrounds.

I'm sure many of you will have had a bit of a row at some time with a complete stranger. Perhaps someone has taken liberties in the local pub, or maybe hit your car and provoked a bit of road rage. None of us are perfect. Everyone loses his or her rag once in a while. Has a friend ever introduced you to someone, and your first impressions have been "What a Pratt this bloke is!" First impressions count for a lot. Once you have got to know them, your suspicions are confirmed. You really clash and want nothing to do with this new-found arse. You really can't get on and the best thing to do is keep away from them. In normal everyday situations that is possible, but in prison you can't do that. You are forced together in what can often be a powder keg environment, where the potential for volatile confrontation is tenfold compared to the outside world.

The staff have to be professional. The prisoners have to do as they are told and bite the bullet. Not very fair, I know, but that is the way it is! Of course both sides, (If that is the right term to use), have ways of lodging a complaint against someone else's bad behaviour. An officer can use the prison rules and regulations to sort out a grievance against a con. For instance, if a con has an outburst at an officer for whatever reason, he may be placed on Governors report. This may result in the con being punished if the charge is proven. Anything from loss of wages or the loss of his T.V. to extra days being added may be awarded.

The con, if he feels he has been treated unfairly, can use the request and complaints system. He will be expected to explain what has happened to him on a form, which generally goes to a Governor. The claim will be investigated and if proven and is serious enough, could eventually lead to an officers dismissal. For more minor infringements, verbal or written warnings will be given. Too many of these, and out you go. These day's thankfully, the need for this kind of action has decreased, as both prisoners and staff are managed better and are under much closer scrutiny.

For a lot of people though, going down the avenue of filling out forms or writing out reports, is not a consideration. Doing it the "proper way", putting it on paper and then waiting, possibly for quite some time, is not an option. What they want is instant retribution. They like to take matters into their own hands. They want to get their own back and enjoy doing it too.

Smith had been on "B" Wing for a couple of years. Most of his adult life had been spent in one of her Majesty's properties and we're not talking palaces or castles here. He was in his forties, but his large body put most of the younger lads to shame. His well-toned and defined muscles were the result of many years of gym sessions, and he was proud of it. He had a presence. No one messed with Smith and Smith messed with no one. He didn't suffer fools easily, and just wanted to do his bird the easy way. His behaviour so far on the wing was good.

Although at the start of sentence he struggled to settle down. His ability to inflict serious damage had not been demonstrated for some time. His reputation alone was enough to keep people at bay.

Mr Brown was an officer with a very similar reputation. The main difference was that Mr Brown liked to put himself about a bit. If he went home at the end of day and he hadn't upset someone, prisoners or staff, he would feel he'd failed. He was what we call in the trade an "Arsehole." Even the staff steered clear of him because trouble was always just round the corner.

He was also a huge man, strong from years of training and fighting. He feared no one and nothing. Various scars stood out between the hard, wrinkled skin of his stern looking face. Short cropped military style hair; tattoos and highly polished boots was the trademark of this menace. The pristine, razor sharp creases in his spotless shirts and trousers were his pride and joy. He was proud of himself and his reputation.

The day he was transferred to "B" Wing was the day a stage was set for a battle of wills, a real clash of the Titan's.

In most jails at this time, slopping out was part of everyday routine. "Slopping out" was a pretty nasty and draconian affair where all internal bodily movements would be collected in a pot overnight. Then all at once, in the morning, the cons would be released in a mass evacuation of topped up pots. This all went down the "Sluice" which was a large drainage system leading to the sewers below. As you can imagine the smell was awful and the day the internal sanitation system was fitted into cells, was a joy for all.

"Potting" was an assault used by many in the old days, where the dubious contents of the pot would be thrown over someone for purposes of retribution. Steady now! Don't get ahead of me. There was strange goings on, going on in "B" Wing at this time.

One evening there was a smell. It was one of the most gag inducing smells officer Jones had the displeasure of enduring. The staff were in the office and this wave came over them, like the dropping of a nuclear bomb and the subsequent fall out.

"What the fuck is that?" someone spluttered.

"Have you dropped your guts again?" said someone else, in Jonesy's direction, as if he could have made a smell like that and still be alive. I think not. He was world renowned for his stinking arse but not as bad as that.

No this was like liquid death. They all piled out of the safety of the office and it hit them again. This wave making the first seem like roses.

"Where the hell is it?" someone ventured through tightly closed lips, looking like a ventriloquist with no dummy. Then Jonesy spotted it or at least the start of it anyway. There down the office spur was a trail of liquid destruction.

The wings accommodation area was made up of three "spurs" or corridors. Each spur contained eight cells, four on either side, making a total of twenty four cells on each landing. They were laid out like a T, left, middle and right. The left spur on the ground floor was not used for accommodating cons but was used for the staff. The cells had been converted into small offices, storerooms, a cloakroom and a tearoom. It was out of bounds to all prisoners and the only thing that separated them from it was a large, locked metal gate reaching from floor to ceiling. Just under the gate, on the worn lino floor, you could see a thick brown liquid. As the staff approached, edging closer and gagging as they went, it became apparent that this was just the start of a very long trail of liquidized poo. This was no ordinary potting, this was shitting up on a military scale. It had been a fantastic strike. Not only had the perpetrator splashed the whole length of our spur with his poo bomb, but most of the office doors were open and had received splash back to their already dirty carpets. This amount of poo can only of come from a bucket and had probably been mixed with a few pints of pee to gain the right consistency. "Jesus Christ" gag, "Who the fuck has done this?" gag gag.

All the cons were banged up, while a well paid volunteer (always from one of the nonce wings) was found to clear up the mess. After rigorous scrubbing, the shit was gone but the smell remained. The staff ripped up the carpets, painted the walls and spent their own money on industrial strength air fresheners but to no avail. It wouldn't budge. For weeks officers found excuses not to do any paperwork. Even the much used tearoom remained empty, while large amounts of coffee addicted staff, found alternatives and gave the spur a wide birth.

Then the second attack came.
Again it occurred during evening association, when all the cons are out. The officers had been extra vigilant. Constantly checking cells for stores of this newly developed chemical weapon, certain that the perpetrator

must have stockpiled his ammo for quite some time in the build up to his first attack. They were sure they would spot it, if not smell it, if any further attempts were made.

This time the main wing office was the unexpected target. As Jonesy pushed open the door, the same vomit inducing smell streamed up his twitching nostrils as it had during the last attack. It instantly rendered him dizzy and light headed. As soon as the brain caught up with the nose, the sick came up.

In the door was a keyhole. He hadn't spotted the dregs of what he had now, unfortunately, discovered coating the office carpet. Somehow, someone had managed to fire a stream of liquidized shit through the keyhole, with enough force to hit the back wall and everything else in between. They later found an old washing up liquid bottle coated in noxious slime that had made the perfect launcher during this latest hit.

Jonesy wasn't sick, he couldn't be. That would have shown a terrible sign of weakness. If he had blown chunks, the cons would have won. They would have succeeded in their attempt to upset the staff. He didn't want to be the one who was deemed to be soft. That would have been terribly embarrassing for him but he was not the one who had done anything wrong. He didn't go round purposefully upsetting people. He was not the target in this mini war, but he thought he knew who was.

This was getting expensive. They carried on for weeks, carpet less, no furniture, stained walls. The wing budget could not stretch to the constant refurbishment's that were needed. The wing was looking more and more like a war zone.

Guards were posted in strategic points to try to catch the serial splasher. Constant watches were needed. The staff had to tighten up the regime and draw up battle plans. Prisoner's movements would have to be restricted. They were determined to stop this nonsense but it carried on. They just didn't have the troops to cover all areas. Smaller hits were made. Dotted around the wing. Some fool accidentally left the staff toilet door open and the excrement terrorists were in and out like ghosts. Like poop carrying Ninja's they hit the loo completely unseen. Rather than just chuck it in haphazardly, they got clever and smeared the walls with a threatening warning. "Fuck you Brown. Get off the wing" it read. This at last confirmed Jonesy's suspicions. Officer Brown had worked his magic and someone was getting him back. He had managed to upset someone so badly that they had resorted to this degrading form of retaliation. On every occasion that the splasher struck, Mr. Brown was on duty but he didn't care. He didn't help with the cleaning up, preferring to sit on his fat arse and watch his fellow staff, the innocent victims, get wrapped up in his war.

Another attack was made. This time a new technique was employed. The chaps had spent some time on research and development and come up with a slow releasing masterpiece. It took a few days to find. The smell was as always, bloody awful but couldn't be located. Staff were looking for the obvious signs of fall out and eventually a cup was spotted on an old disused speaker, which was a remnant from an old intercom system. Located high on a seldom seen wall, the upside down cup that had contained the poo, had been gradually drip, drip, dripping its obnoxious contents onto a low lying stalagmite of crap.

"When will it stop?" people would often say with an almost beaten sound to their voices. There wasn't long to wait.

The final blow was struck only a couple of days after the dripping incident. Mr. Brown was on duty this morning and was sitting on the landing letting the other staff run around as usual. There had been a particularly heated discussion the night before, between Smith and Brown, and everyone realised it wouldn't be long before they came to blows.

As Jonesy walked around unlocking the doors he was thinking how quiet it was that morning. Everyone was coming out of their cells, but the daily emptying of pots didn't seem to have started with its usual gusto. Usually this is the first thing that happens. Everyone wants the dirty pot out of the cell and down the sluice. Today was different. Then he realised why. Quick as flash, Smith shot out of his cell like an Exocet Missile carrying a deadly cargo programmed to seek and destroy. There was nothing the staff could do. He hurtled round the corner, a man on a mission, fuelled by anger, guided by hatred, straight at Mr. Brown. His one sole aim was to humiliate him, to assault him in a way he wouldn't forget. He was going to finish this war once and for all and topple his tormentor. Mr. Brown spotted him. The sudden realisation that an imminent attack was approaching showed on his very worried face. He didn't get up, he didn't have time. At only an arm's length away Smith unleashed his load and tipped the bucket and its contents directly onto the head of his target. Time stood still. He had got him. Weeks and weeks of constant torment had finally taken their toll. Smith was not to be messed with. He had got his revenge. This was the final act of his pre-planned campaign. Mr. Brown would never live this down. He would look foolish in front of the gathered witnesses.

But the bastard didn't move. There was no explosive roar as he ran screaming to the showers in a flurry of convulsive retching. He just sat there with the bucket on his head, covered from head to toe in liquid shit. It was everywhere. The smell was unbelievable. Fighting back the sick, the assembled officer's stood motionless looking at Smith, not knowing what to do, and waiting for Mr. Brown's reaction.

Then he twitched. His arms reached skyward and his shit covered hands tried to get a grip on the bucket. As he raised it, small lumps of rancid poo freed themselves from the suction caused by the tightness of the bucket and dribbled down his chest. His perfect uniform left unrecognisable under the layer of stagnant diarrhoea. Painfully slowly the bucket was lifted, until his face came into view for the first time in what seemed like hours. Jonesy would never forget his words. As the bits fell from his ears, nose and chin and he gently and calmly spat out the bits that had found their way into his now silent mouth. He wiped away the excess from his lips and said a slow, calm and sarcastic way ,
"Smith, have you been eating Sausages?"

This was not what anyone expected to hear! The bastard had won! He showed no emotion, no signs of aggression and spoke in a soft, controlled voice. As the staff grabbed Smith and removed him to the Segregation Unit, he looked on still in a state of shock at his apparent failure to upset Mr. Brown. Only once Smith had gone did Mr. Brown leap up and run to the showers and still dripping shit, he shouted,

"I knew I'd find out who was doing it. I knew I'd get him off the wing."

Mr. Brown was victorious!!

Butter Ears

Smith was a compete dick and everybody knew it! Even Smith knew it. He said he had ADHD but that was never proved and no record of it was ever noted in his medical file. He was just a childish, badly behaved, get involved with everything dick! He was just 21 and had been sent to big boys prison as quickly as possible as he was causing havoc in the Young Offenders prison where he was previously held. He was what you would call a problem child. Coming from a broken home with a family who had all done time, he had no manners, no idea how to behave, no role models and generally no fucking idea!

Big for his age with a very short skinhead, badly squashed nosed and it has to be said, huge jug ears, he was a formidable looking young man. He had fought continuously throughout his various sentences and wore the scars of many battles. He was scared of nothing and no one and even now in the adult system he was generally feared by staff and prisoners alike.

 Whenever anything happened on the wing you could guarantee he was involved in some way. Some more experienced, older and wiser prisoners would often use him to do their dirty work. Collecting drug debts, lending tobacco and getting twice as much back (often referred to as Double Bubble) and unleashing violence on other prisoners who had crossed his "Employers" were daily tasks he carried out. He had little or no regard for prison rules and would often be caught by staff up to his games and spent many days in the Seg unit.

One morning officer Jones was doing his daily L.B.B checks. This stood for Locks Bolts and Bars, where the assigned officer would go into every cell on his wing and check to make sure that all locks, bolts, bars and the general fabric of the cell were both intact and not tampered with. Not many officers enjoyed doing this job as it was monotonous, time consuming and was often met with abuse from prisoners every time you stepped into their domain. Many of them had rugs or carpets on the floor and they hated officers stepping on them with their big dirty boots. Of course they were seldom dirty but the cons would claim anything for a row with staff.

On this particular morning though Jonesy laid eyes on a sight he had not seen before. Smith was bending over at his window and appeared to have his head sticking out of it. Prisoners often stuck their heads out the windows at night so they could chat easily with their neighbour or even someone a distance away but Jonesy had never actually found a prisoner doing it during the day and leaving themselves in such a vulnerable position. Strangely though, Smith appeared to be crying.

"You alright Smithy?" Officer Jones ventured but there was no response.

"Smithy! Are you alright?" he shouted fearing he couldn't be heard.

"Who the fucks that?" shouted Smithy startled by someone's presence behind him.

"It's me, Officer Jones. What you doing with your head out the window?"

"Taking in the scenery! What do you think I'm doing? I've got my fucking head stuck you Pratt! Get me out of here!"

Jonesy told him to stop being stupid and get his head out as he thought it was just another of Smith's stupid pranks.

"I'm not Messing about Gov. My heads really stuck, I can't get it out."

He sounded a bit desperate and Jonesy thought he may of been telling the truth but wasn't sure as this was silly Smith after all.

"OK Smithy, I'll go and get some help" said the officer as he walked out of the cell. He then waited just outside the cell half expecting Smith to come running out giggling at his little prank.

Peering back in he found Smith in the same position and his legs were starting to tremble from standing in the same position for so long.

"You're still there then Smithy. Can't you get your head out?"

"For fuck sake! Are you fucking stupid? I'm stuck and it hurts Gov you gotta do something"

At this point, it struck Jonesy that Smith does have an unusually large head and of course those massive ears, so believed that he could actually be as stuck as he says.

"Wait there Smith, I'll go and get someone."

"WAIT HERE!! Are you taking the piss? Where the fuck am I gonna go? My heads stuck!!"

Five minutes later the officer posse returned, laughed, discussed the course of action, laughed some more and decided to get some butter to spread round Smiths big head to help slide it out of the frame.

Prison windows are not the easiest things to use. Especially if you're trying to get your head in or out.

They are made up of many small panes with reinforced steel between the glass. There is only one opener and that is in the middle of the rest. Most of these opening windows have either been broken off or smashed so many times they are no longer replaced. They are small too, so small I wouldn't want to risk poking my head through one. Also many of the outer, smaller panes on this particular window had been broken so rather than replace the whole lot the works department, to save money, had stuck a huge piece of clear Perspex over the whole area with a hole cut out of the centre to access the opener. This had been so firmly fixed that it was impossible to reach Smith's head through any of the other panes.

The butter arrived, or rather the stuff that the prison uses as butter. It tastes like axel grease and the Prison probably buys the small portions for a £1 a thousand and reluctantly dishes them out to prisoners as if it was gold. Amid a flourish of expletives from Smith, Jonesy slid his skinny fingers and hands through the gaps in the window and liberally smeared this yellow goo all over Smith's neck, ears and head, thoroughly enjoying his task as if it was payback for all the grief he'd taken since Smith's arrival.

Next they told Smith to ease back slowly and try to slide his slimy head back through the frame. It didn't happen, Smithy was squealing like a bitch. The assembled Officers still weren't sure if he was actually trying to remove his head or if he was just causing a scene for the fun of it. So they decided some extra pressure would be in order. A couple of them took a firm hold of Smithy's broad shoulders and gradually increased the pressure and pulled away from the window. Still no movement but loads of screaming and a few tears from Smith. He really was stuck.

Someone phoned the works department to see if they could help but they were busy as usual and short staffed as they always seemed to be. The one thing that was really needed was a ladder but for obvious reasons that's the one thing that you don't usually find lying around a prison.

Jonesy reached through and applied some more butter hoping that a good thick layer would help. The more they pulled the more agitated Smithy got and the worse the situation became. He was stuck but he was also resisting against the pull of the Officers as the more they tugged at his shoulders the more pain he felt. After an hour or so a wise old P.O. (Principal Officer) arrived. He had been in the service for more years than the five or so assembled Officers had between them. He had seen it all and also knew Smith rather well. On the numerous occasions Smith had been taken to the Block, this P.O. had been present on most of them and really didn't like Smith at all. He pondered the situation for a while and knew what to do. He knew that Smithy had a real fear of being raped in Prison. He had numerous conversations with the youngster and had learnt that this had happened a few times to other Young Offenders at his previous Prison and his old mates had wound him up saying it would happen to him when he goes to an adult prison as he would be the youngest one there and the old lags would abuse him. The P.O asked for hush and told the Officers to leave the cell. He added volume to his voice so that a now quiet Smith could clearly hear him.

"I'm going to do something to you Smith that I've been wanting to do for a long time."

Smith could just about see into the cell from outside the window by craning his neck round a bit. The P.O. continued,

"Since your arrival in my Prison, you have caused me untold amounts of grief and to be honest I have wanted to kick your arse on numerous occasions. But over the last couple of months I have noticed a different side of you and I have become rather fond of you. So much so that I really have started to fancy you. You are a very good looking lad and you have a great body."

Smith was deadly silent and very still for a change.

The P.O. reached down and slowly undone the zip on the flies of his trousers. The Officers outside could clearly hear that slow rasping sound as the zip was provocatively lowered. They thought he had gone mad!

Smith on the other hand was going mad! He had also heard the zip coming down and could clearly see the P.O. reaching inside for his genitals. Smithy was screaming like a baby.

As quick as a flash and with the loss of a fair bit of ear skin, Smith yanked his head back out of the window and stood screaming to the staff to get the P.O. out of the his cell.

The P.O. calmly opened the door and walked out, with a wry smile on his face he uttered,

"My work here is done! Take that dick down the Seg, he'll be gone tomorrow."

Escape Pack

There are a multitude of escorts a prisoner can go on.
Transfer to another prison, hospital appointments, lifer
town visits (where lifers are taken to a town with no
cuffs, to do shopping, eating etc to help them reintegrate
after many years in prison). Home visits, to see sick or
dying close relatives, to attend funerals. To visit a rehab
or probation backed establishment that offers places of
help to the newly released prisoner. The list goes on and
it is usually down to the prison officers to arrange these
escorts, and then take the cons out wherever they need to
go.
 Usually the prisoner is cuffed to an officer for the
duration of the escort. This is to ensure the means of
escape are kept to a minimum and the prisoner is
returned safely to continue his sentence. Sometimes they
do not go to plan and escapes do occur.
Then there are un-cuffed escorts which only usually
happen when the prisoner has already served a large
percentage of his sentence and has built up a high level of
trust among the officers and Governors. Or they are
category "D" Prisoners. These guys are generally in for
minor crimes and are deemed little or no risk to the
public.

Smith had been in for ages and although he had said and
done all the right things as far as the management were
concerned, the staff all thought he was an arse and should
not be trusted. He was a tall thin guy with straggly
blonde hair and would not look out of place at a 60's
flower power party. His clothes echoed the era with tie
dyed shirts and flared cords and sandals, a wispy Goatee

completed the look and to all he looked like a peace loving hippie but some of the officers knew better. He had an explosive temper and although he generally managed to hide it well, a couple of the officers had experienced it first hand and kept him at arm's length. Somehow he managed to win the trust of a couple of Governors. He was asking for help with his ongoing recovery from drugs and was looking for a day out. On interview he ticked all the right boxes as far as they were concerned and was considered a low risk and the arrangements were to be made for Smiths escort to a Drug rehab in his home area. This was for both sides, the counsellors and Smith the druggy, to decide if they were right for each other and could ultimately work together.

"Are they fucking mad!?" shouted Jonesy who was Smithy's personal officer and had just been told of the plans for his imminent temporary release.
"The bloke's a fucking idiot. He'll run as soon as he gets out the fucking Taxi."
Not only had Smith blagged a visit to a rehab in his home town, he had been granted a licence and would go escorted by an officer with no cuffs. Basically the licence would list the things he can and can't do and states the time he can go out and the time he must be back. If he fails to return by the stated time he will be unlawfully at large and could get more time inside if disciplinary charges are laid. That's if he was ever seen again!

Most of the staff that really knew Smith were of the same opinion. The Governors involved with this one were really gonna come unstuck with this hot spud. But it fell to Jonesy as the personal officer, to make all the arrangements which he did professionally as always. Although he was worried about what might happen on the day of the escort.

Part of the arrangements meant liaising with the security department. They would check out the establishment to be visited, arrange the transport and write the licence conditions to be signed by the Governor. They would also write and supply the escape pack. This is a sealed envelope, to be carried by the escorting officer and would only be opened in an emergency I.E. Escape. In the envelope would be photos of the prisoner, a very detailed description of him including hair colour, eye colour, facial details, height, weight, tattoos, distinguishing marks etc. Also home address details, family & known associate address details. Practically anything that could be of use to the police once the escape had been reported to them. Obviously any information contained in the envelope could be extremely important to assist in the runaway's immediate re-capture.

The day of the escort arrived. Smith was excited and upbeat. Jonesy was well pissed off. Although he had been the main organiser of the escort he had hoped that he would not actually be called on to accompany Smith on this jolly to the re-hab. So it was with much disgust and disappointment that Jonesy saw his detail that morning and he was in fact the chosen one to escort this scumbag out for the day.

From the moment they strapped into the prison car, Jonesy felt this feeling of impending doom. That was a phrase Jonesy often used having first heard it on a first aid course a few years previous. It was a lesson about heart attacks, when after reeling off a huge list of

possible symptoms for spotting a heart attack the
instructor said,

"The one sure way to know if the person is having a heart
attack is if they have a feeling of impending doom!"
Jonesy envisaged asking future patients if they are
experiencing a feeling of impending doom and getting
one of two answers,

1. Not really but my left arm is very numb = No
    Heart Attack
2. AARRrrggghhhhh = No Heart Attack

   NO impending doom = No heart attack!!

Instead Jonesy liked to use this gem of diagnostic
knowledge to describe the feeling he got when he was
given details or jobs he really didn't want to do. The jobs
that made you wonder why you joined the prison service.
The days that made you wish you had thrown a sickie.
This was brought on by the security S.O.s comments just
before he collected Smith to take him to the car.

 "We've had information that Smith is going to run away
today!" said the very serious looking S.O.

 "So why am I still taking him?" was Jonesy's obvious
and reasonable reply.

 "The bloke's on licence. The Governor says he can still
go as the licence has been signed. If he runs, you can't
stop him Jonesy coz he's allowed to go anywhere, within
reason, as long as he gets back by the time stated on the
licence".

 "So what do I do if he goes?"

 "Let him!" the S.O. said with not a touch of irony in his
voice. "If you can, monitor where he goes but make sure

you go to the nearest police station and report the abscond".

"Fucking great! Thanks lads", said Jonesy as he left the security office clutching the paperwork he needed and dragging the black cloud that was forming above his head.

"Put your seatbelt on Smith, I'd hate to see you go through the windscreen", lied Jonesy as they pulled away in the blue prison Astra. As he drove he could detect a change in Smith. He could feel the atmosphere changing. Although there was no dialect he could sense that things were going wrong already. He glanced across at the con. He looked the same but he kept picturing in his mind a scene from a Jekyll and Hyde film and saw Smithy transmogrifying into a complete and utter tit instead of just the normal tit he was before they left. They parked at their destination and Jonesy found he was right.

"OK Smith, we've got a little while till your appointment, shall we go for a cup of tea or look round the shops?" the troubled officer said hopefully.

"Fuck that! I'm going to the pub for a pint."

"But you're not allowed to go into a public house, it says so on the licence!"

"I don't give a shit! You can nick me if you like and we'll sort it out when we get back to the prison. What will they do, give me a few extra days? It will be worth it. I ain't been pissed for years!" said the defiant horrible one.

Oh dear thought Jonesy to himself. I'm going to draw my stave and batter the bastard! But he knew he couldn't as Smith was on licence and Jonesy was already losing control.

Smith had been given money for food by the prison and had also been allowed to bring some of his own private cash with him. This money is sent by friends or family for the con to spend in the prison shop or to by goods from Argos or M&M's that kind of mail order type place. How much they could spend would largely depend on how they behaved. Standard cons could use about £15 a week. Basic cons (naughty boys) could only spend a fiver and enhanced lads (good boys) up to £25. Mind you some of the more successful Bank Robbers or Drug Dealers used to use these accounts to launder quite large amounts of money. Sums of £500 a week were not unusual and the freshly released con could walk out with thousands of pounds on a nice clean Home Office cheque. Well that's how it looked anyway.

 Smith had a fair few quid on him and looked hell bent on having a good session. He even offered to buy the first round! Of course Jonesy accompanied him in to the rough looking hostelry but only to keep an eye on him and only accepted an Orange Juice. He felt sure Smith would soon run and didn't want to breath beer on the desk sergeant as he reported the escape.

Looking around the inside of the pub, Jonesy wished he had stayed outside. It was so rough even the arms on the chairs had Tattoo's! Would there be an accomplice in here? Someone to help Smith get away, maybe to grab Jonesy while Smith made off on his toes? Jonesy scrutinised all the rough looking sorts that came through the door, while trying to discourage Smith from going back and forth to the bar. He was up and down like a whore's drawers. After years of alcohol starvation there was no stopping Smith and copious amounts of beer were soon taking affect. He even started saying things like, "I think I might just fuck off you know!" or "What you gonna do if I run? Fuck all!"

Jonesy kept his composure and ignored Smiths baiting but shit himself when Smithy inevitably, finally walked out to the gents.

Oh shit! Will he come back? Should I follow him? Is he gonna leg it now? Jonesy decided to stand by the toilet door to keep an eye. What if he climbs out the window? He decided to go in.

"I ain't going anywhere yet Gov. I ain't pissed yet!" said Smith as he pushed past on his way back to the bar and back to the drinking. The appointment was fast approaching and Jonesy was getting anxious. He was also very surprised when Smithy stood up and said,

"Come on then let's go and see these druggies! Just going for a slash first."

Here we go again. Jonesy thought this was it again. He'll go out the window and make him look foolish. But still he came back, much to Jonesy's surprise. The re-hab was only a short walk for a sober person but Smithy looked worse for wear and was wobbling along the path abusing passersby. But then whhooooof..........It was like a starting pistol had been fired and Smith was out the blocks and flying. Jonesy couldn't believe his eyes. The tottering piss head had gone in the blink of an eye, down a narrow side street and away before Jonesy could say,

"You cheeky, Shandy drinking Fucker!" That was the only explanation Jonesy could rationalise. That Smith had actually had ten pints of Shandy or alcohol free beer and had put on his drunken display to take away any suspicion he would be capable of legging it. He picked his spot to run pretty well as he knew the area and disappeared down a warren of backstreets.

Jonesy was not having a good day. So it was with a fair amount of trepidation that he sauntered into the local cop shop.

"I'd like to report the escape of a prisoner, well technically an abscond" said the plain clothed man in front of the desk sergeant.

"I'm sorry?" said the puzzled officer of the law.

"So am I" said Jonesy and then attempted to explain himself and suddenly remembered the escape pack in his jacket pocket. Ah! that would be useful. That would give the policeman all he needed to know. It would have a photo, a personal description, any known addresses locally and all the relevant security information. Jonesy handed him the envelope. The Sergeant looked blankly at Jonesy and threw the piece of paper onto the desk. Jonesy's day suddenly got a whole lot worse when he looked down at this;

SECURITY RESTRICTED

NAME...SMITH
PRISON No...............................NF2121
D.O.B...25/07/75

HEIGHT......................................Not known
WEIGHT......................................Not known
FACE SHAPE............................Not known
HAIR COLOUR.........................Not known
EYE COLOUR...........................Not known
BUILD...Not known
TATTOOS..................................Not known
DISTINGUIHING MARKS....Not known

```
┌──────────────┐
│              │
│    PHOTO     │
│     NOT      │
│  AVAILABLE   │
│              │
│              │
└──────────────┘
```

ADDRESS................................Not known

NEXT OF KIN...........................Not known

NOTE
* THIS MAN CAN BE HIGHLY DANGEROUS. MAY TRY TO ESCAPE IF GIVEN THE CHANCE TO DO SO*

I Want A Light!!

It was a normal day. One of those days that seemed to drag by like it was two days long. It had been a normal morning and now it was a normal afternoon. In fact it had been a pretty normal week!

Most days were like this in prison. The stuff you see on the telly is rubbish. All over dramatised tosh that the producers want you to believe actually happens. About the most accurate portrayal of prison life so far was Porridge. The main reason this did so well is because of the humour. Most officers have a pretty good sense of humour. Most of the prisoners do too. Sure the job has its bad side. There are always those that are looking for trouble, on both sides, in fact. I certainly won't try to hide that. But on the whole, the roof stayed on because everyone could share a good laugh together.

Every now and again though the shit did hit the fan. You had to be ready at any time to deal with any situation that arose. Things could turn violent in the blink of an eye. So the odd boring day or week was nothing to be sniffed at.

This normal day would soon change though. There must have been someone blinking a hell of a lot somewhere.

Smith was in the Segregation Unit. These are generally very grim places. Where all the rules are strictly adhered too. It's where people are held away from other prisoners for various reasons. In this case Smith was on a "lie down". This generally happens when unruly prisoners that can't settle down on normal location in one of the wings, become so hard to deal with it is necessary to lock them on their own, for their safety and the safety of those around them. Usually this kind of prisoner becomes such a drain on resources that they are moved from prison to prison, so fresh staff can try to handle them and bring them back in line. If they don't get on with staff at one prison, they may click with an officer at the next. Sometimes they even spend their whole sentence on this roller coaster ride if they are so badly behaved, and simply will not conform. For them, the Seg is usually the end of the line.

Smith was one of these men. He was known throughout the system and had been in almost every prison in the area. Staff were very wary of this man. He had a reputation for being very volatile and could inflict serious injury without batting an eye.

He was of average build and average height but that's where the normality's ended. He was incredibly strong. His well-trained physique looked like a roman marble statue with its well-defined abs'. He was fast too. He was able to launch off his bed and be in a ready position as soon as he heard the key in the lock. Always alert and ever ready. That was Smith.

Prisoners like this were treated with caution. There had to be a minimum of three staff on duty in the Seg just to open his door. Most of the time like all other con's he was fine, but Smith had that bit more potential to cause trouble. And when he did, it was usually bad.

There was three staff on duty this day like any other. Mr. Jones was one of them, accompanied by Mr. Brown and Mr. White. All had been in for a number of years and worked in the Seg because they knew how to deal with awkward prisoners. They were all big lads too, as Seg staff tended to be. They were milling about, as usual, going about their business, as they do, when there was a loud bang from down one of the spurs. (A spur is a sort of corridor that the cell doors open on to.) This was not unusual because the prisoners in the Seg had learnt that the bell was for emergencies only, and if they were to use it for the wrong reason they would find themselves on Governors report. If they wanted to attract staff's attention for something menial they should knock on their door and someone would be along shortly. There was another loud bang. Then another.

Jones raised an eyebrow as the loud thuds in the distance started to take on a consistent rhythm.

"Is that bloody Smith?" asked Brown. There wasn't many con's in the Seg that day so he had a pretty good idea it would be.

"I'll go and see in a minute," said White; "I'll just finish my tea."

Boom. Boom. Boom. Went the cell door and the noise suggested there was a matter of urgency from where ever the banging originated. Mixed in with the loud booms the officers could make out a voice but couldn't quite hear what it was saying. It was sort of singing!

"Go and see what that nutter wants? He's starting to wind me up," Says Jonesy becoming agitated by the unnecessary noise.

Brown got up from writing a report and walked casually to Smith's door.

"What do you want Smith", he asked in a, I'm sick to death of being here in this boring, nothing ever happens job, kind of way.

"I.... want.... a.... light," chants Smith in tune to his own banging.

"And I.... haven't..... got...... one." declares Brown and joined in with the tune.

"I.... want..... a...... light," repeats Smith as his voice and banging got louder, but Brown was already on his way back to the wing office.

"What did he want", asked Jones, not really interested but happy to make conversation.

"Says he wants a light for his cigarette"

"Tell him we haven't got one."

"I already did."

"Have you got a light Mr. White?" asked Jonesy.

"No I don't smoke, and if I did I wouldn't give one to that aggravating bastard."

"Well he's shit it then, just ignore him. He'll get bored soon."

Did he hell. The banging and chanting got louder. Boom. Boom. Boom. "I.... want..... a....... light." Boom. Boom. Boom. "I.... want..... a..... light."

Ten minutes eased into twenty. Half an hour merged into an hour and still Smith persisted. Louder and louder. Boom. Boom. Boom. "I..... want..... a..... light."

"Go and have a word with that twat will you?" said Jonesy, he's really getting on my nerves now.

"Look Smith we've already told you, we don't smoke and we haven't got a light, and anyway if we did you couldn't have it, you set fire to your own cell last week. Remember?" Mr. White tried to reason. "Now be a good egg and give it a rest, you're agitating the other prisoners."

Boom. Boom. Boom. "I.... want..... a..... light", was shouted again and again from behind the door. White looked through the spy hole and could see that much of Smiths furniture, (which was made of cardboard in the Seg) had been smashed and his cell was now slowly filling with water as the taps flowed at full pelt and the toilet had been blocked.

He called the others to have a look.

"For Christ's sake. This is getting stupid." Said Jonesy, the more senior of the officers on duty.

"Turn off the taps and behave yourself Smith" he shouted through the closed door. But Smith couldn't hear him. It was too late. He had got himself going now and there was no stopping him. He was hearing but wasn't listening. He meant business. His temper had been lost and he was not going to stop until he got what he wanted.

What had started out as a persistent pain in the arse that could have been dealt with in a second or two had now escalated to a potentially dangerous incident.

Boom. Boom. Boom. "I..... want.... a...... light." Smith carried on beating out his rhythm. But now he was serious. He was spitting through gritted teeth. In between banging the door he would turn round and throw something across his cell. Most of the items in there were smashed and all the while he shouted at the top of his voice,

"I..... WANT..... A...... LIGHT!!"

There wasn't much the staff could do at this point. They couldn't open the door or they would obviously have a fight on their hands. They were wishing they had found a light a couple of hours ago. The duty Governor would have to be informed, extra staff would be called in and Smith would have to be removed from his cell by a team of staff dressed in full riot kit and he would be placed in a special cell. This was designed to hold violent prisoners who were hell bent on attacking staff or prison property and contained nothing more than a concrete plinth to sleep on and a very sturdy metal toilet, firmly bolted to the floor. Using this facility was not taken lightly and had to be performed to the letter. The correct procedures had to be followed and a lot of paperwork was involved.

The Governor arrived and instantly heard the demands. It was hard to ignore.

"I... want...... a..... light. I..... want..... a....... light." Boom. Boom. Boom. Boom. Boom. Boom.

"What's the matter with this man?" asked the Governor somewhat naively.

"He wants a light sir", said Jones with a stiff upper lip.

"How long has this been going on", asks the Governor, who was a rather small pathetic little man with a backbone made of rubber.

"Oh, a couple of hours now sir."

"Well why don't you go in and give him a light then?" questioned the Governor.

"With all due respect sir, Smith is a very dangerous man. He is very manipulative and if I know Smith, he's after something else. We don't trust him sir. He has smashed his cell up and the only course of action I recommend is to send in a team to remove him."

"Nonsense", says the Governor. "I have a lighter here and I want you to go and give it to him"

A look of horror descended across the faces of the assembled officers. Some of which were now dressed in full riot gear and were raring to go.

"I don't think that's a good idea Gov. He's worked himself up into a frenzy. Someone could get hurt. Plus he set alight to another cell last week. There is more to this

Sir and I don't want to give in to him now", said Jones, now seriously concerned that not only will someone get hurt but that Smith will actually get what he has been demanding. And that just wouldn't do. That means he will have won!

"I am telling you to go and give him the lighter", the Governor repeated.

"Why don't you give it to him Governor", says Jones in a stand of defiance. And much to everyone's amazement the Governor said he would!

"Alright. I will", said the Governor.

So through the assembled staff he strode, to the shaking door of Smith. The sound of the Governor's rattling bones could be heard above the sound of the pounding and Smith's continued chants of,

"I.... want...... a..... light. I...... want....... a........ light."

"Smith. It's the Governor. I'm going to give you this lighter. Will you behave," squeaked the Governor. The staff all waited for a loud "Fuck Off" but it didn't come. Instead Smith said,

"Yes Governor." He spoke quietly for the first time in hours.

The smug Governor looked round at the assembled masses, with a look on his face that said "punch me I'm a smug bastard."

"Officer open this door," Said the Governor. Now with a chest as bloated as his ego. Single handily he had brought this situation to a quiet conclusion and had avoided a major incident.

 The door was very carefully opened. Like a Bulldozer it swept aside the carnage that was once Smiths belongings. Smith appeared at the door totally knackered from his exertions but still dangerous and the lighter was passed in. The door was then slammed shut, and the game was over. The Governor paraded around like a General who had just one a battle. Like a male Lion in charge of his pride.

Then all too soon his world crumbled around him as the noise returned like a recurring nightmare.

Boom. Boom. Boom. Boom. Boom. Boom.

But this time the chant changed, and the Governor cringed as all assembled heard the words,

"I want a Fag! I want a Fag!!"

For anyone reading this in the U.S. Fag is a common slang word in the UK for Cigarette. He did not suddenly require a gay man!

It's in the Bag

The visits area can be a volatile place but can also throw up its fair share of amusing stories. One such day the security department had received information that a drug pass was going to be made.

The whole visiting room is monitored by CCTV cameras with every corner being watched. Also all the visits staff are in touch with the camera operator via radios with earpieces, so if anything is spotted the staff can respond instantly. Due to the security info that had been received, all the staff were being extra vigilant and were quite edgy, waiting for some signs of a pass.

There are various ways a pass can occur. The visitor, if female, will bring the drugs into the room secreted in an area where the sun doesn't shine. (Mind you the way some of their girls dressed and paraded around the hall, they thought the sun really shone from this area!)
Once in the room she would casually and discretely remove it from her nether regions and will pass it to the con by dropping it in a cup of tea, placing it in a packet of crisps or placing it straight into his hand. He will then either swallow it or plug it. Plugging it involves parts of his body similar to the parts she used to bring the stuff through in the first place. The Vagina and Anus are very commonly used as storage areas within the prison system. Contrary to popular belief you would never see a prison officer slipping on a pair of latex gloves to give a prisoner a quick internal. It is simply not allowed. Only a doctor can perform this dubious duty. Drugs can be bought in, in reasonably small amounts, quite successfully using this method, as the officers cannot

retrieve it from any body orifices so there is only a very small window of opportunity to grab it as it goes from hole to hole in just a few seconds. Even though these holes aren't huge you would be amazed how much can be stored in this receptacle. These days, with the latest seizures showing an increase in coke and crack finds, the dealing can be very lucrative for those stupid enough to risk a prison sentence. Any visitors caught bringing drugs into the prison using any method could face many years inside themselves if found guilty in court.

There was a bit of banter going on across the radio between the members of visits staff. Jones was not amused though and had his sights firmly fixed on the table being targeted that day. He was oblivious to the conversations going on around him. He wanted to catch these people doing their drug smuggling and he wanted it bad.

For some time now the visits S.O. had been discussing, with another member of staff about the whereabouts of the date stamp. This was used to stamp the forms that visitors used to prove they had been up on any particular day. These forms were used to claim travelling expenses for the visit. Anyway, it was in the bag that security sends down with all the radios used for visits. Trying to make himself heard over all the noise in the hall was useless, so he pressed the transmit button on his radio and said,

"It's in the bag!"

That was all Jonesy needed to hear. Like an Exocet missile he launched from his seat in the direction of the target table. He had been given the command. At the very same moment Smith, on the target table, picked up a packet of crisps and delved in a hand probably to remove a crisp for eating purposes. But in Jonesy's eyes he was retrieving some drugs. "It's in the bag!" He had heard. Someone must have seen something go in the crisp packet. He flew over the table grabbing the packet in one hand and Smithy's neck in the other, fearing he had already tried to swallow it. The whole place fell silent, everyone wondering what the hell Jonesy was doing. The crash of officers and prisoners bones on wall and floor was deafening. The look of horror on the S.O.'s face as he realised the mistake as Jonesy stood up triumphantly with a bag of crushed Cheese and Onion in his clenched fist was a picture. Jonesy's face soon matched that of the S.O. as the realisation of what he had done slowly dawned on him as his chuckling colleagues looked on instead of running to assist him in the removal of his target. To save face Jonesy continued in his quest for a result and bullied Smith out of the hall, claiming he had seen a pass that not even the camera operator had spotted. He had some explaining to do that afternoon.

<u>Saucy!</u>

He was a tall, strong looking man for his age. In his late seventies at a guess, but still looked good. He was from a military background, and looked like something from Dads Army. His rounded shoulders slumping forward slightly gave him the look he was carrying the world on them. With long, thick hairs sticking out of his protruding eyebrows he had the air of a typical granddad. Dressed in prison clothes, slightly crumpled and musty, he drew no attention to himself in the crowd of prisoners he generally sat with.

But there was a darker side to this man. One that the staff would never have seen if this cruel series of events had never took place. A strange turn up for the books that turned this fine upstanding member of the prison community into a laughing stock for many months…

One night, at about 11:00hrs a buzzer sounded on the three's landing on "D" wing. Not such an unusual occurrence, prisoners habitually press their emergency call button for the stupidest of reasons. Signs all over the wing state that the button is for emergency use only, and still they press it. If you put signs up on the wing telling them to press their buzzer at every opportunity, you would probably be called upstairs less, such is the mentality of most prisoners. You see, as soon as a buzzer sounds, it must be treated as a potential emergency and be checked out straight away. After being called upstairs about fifteen times in an hour to turn off ten cell lights, pass three papers, tell someone to turn down their stereo, and one "sorry Gov.' I thought it was the light switch", the old "Cry Wolf" scenario starts to come into play. But on this occasion the officer was on the ball, and what a shock he got.

The officer on duty that night was one of the old school. He had been in for years. He was tall and sturdy with a gruff manner. He didn't suffer fools easily and was well known for his no nonsense approach. Officer Jones had survived riots and assaults galore and there was nothing this guy hadn't seen, he thought. Until tonight!
At this time of the night he was in no mood for messing about. He slid across the cover of the spy hole after cancelling the sound of the buzzer and was met with a completely new vision. One that he would probably never see again if he lived to be a thousand. There in the corner of the rather shabby looking cell was Smith, appearing very embarrassed and as naked as the day he was born. Going with the strange situation, Jonesy asked Smith what was going on.
Now, remember that Smith was ex-Army. When you read his sections of speech, it will be much more realistic and will recreate the scene perfectly, if you read in a kind of well-to-do, military family background sort of accent.
So, back to the action!
"What do you want?" says Jonesy. He struggled to make himself heard above the usual evening din that occurred on most wings. This included prisoners shouting messages to each other and the catastrophic sound that is made when ten different stereos blast out ten different songs at the same time.
"It's a bit embarrassing," says Smith looking more sheepish as the seconds since initial contact slip by and turn into minutes.

"What is wrong?" repeats Jonesy becoming more agitated during the same seconds and minutes.

"I don't really want to shout it out," declares Smith.

"Stop fucking about Smith and tell me what's wrong?" says the ever patient Officer Jones.

At this point Jonesy notices that Smiths hand is firmly lodged behind his back.

"What have you got behind your back Smith? What the hell is going on?" says Jonesy completely ignoring his nudity as if it was the most normal thing to see. I mean, you see seventy-year-old geezers walking about nude all the time. Don't you?

"Could you please open the door? I don't want to shout it out." Says Smith, now with a pitiful tone and close to tears and Jonesy realised, for the first time, that something was really wrong.

You can't just go opening doors in the middle of the night. It is after all a prison and even in emergency situations a degree of security had to be maintained. You have to have more staff on hand in case of trouble so Jonesy sauntered off to seek the advice and guidance of his Senior Officer.

Back at the door the two officers and the night patrol chap (a civilian worker that patrols the wings but carries no keys) continued their bizarre line of questioning.

"What have you got behind your back Smith? And why are you standing in the nude?" His hand seemed to be at about bum level and had not moved an inch since he was found.

"Please open the door and I'll tell you."

A rapid assessment of the situation was made and it was decided that three members of staff against a nude 70-year-old pensioner were pretty good odds. If he kicked off they could probably take him. The door was duly opened. All to soon the full horrors of the situation were revealed. Well they were explained. Well, read on.

"What's wrong Smith?" says the S.O.

"I have a tomato sauce bottle stuck up my arse!" he whispered.

"What?"

"I have a tomato sauce bottle stuck up my arse!!" he whispered again, leaning in to the officer's ear as he didn't want to have to say that out loud.

A look of collective disbelief and silence fell among the gathered officers.

"Bollocks!" says Jonesy.

"No just the bottle" says Smith.

At this point there is a need to go into the very probable reason for this perverse and rather dodgy behaviour. I have learnt since that date that men have a thing called the Prostate Gland, (shaped rather like a donut), secreted about their person, well more precisely, inside the anus, which when stimulated can produce an orgasm. Apparently, after years of self-abuse, the only way this dirty old bugger could get off sexually, was to poke his donut with whatever item came to hand. Hence the bottle!

But, and it is a very big but! Smith did not poke the neck of this, (I don't want to advertise here, and I'm not trying to suggest the best kind of bottle to use in this case), hexagonal shaped, tomato flavoured, male dildo into the murky depths. He poked it up thick end first!! I suppose he liked to use the thin end as a handle.

Now your eyes have stopped watering. Get this. Once inserted and during whatever act he was involved in at the time, he had a major muscle spasm and his well worked ring piece clenched the bottle in right up to the neck. Panic set in and the bottle was locked fast. Fearing for his own safety and obviously wanting to get the foreign object out of his ass, he inserted his finger into the end of the bottle to assist in its removal and that got stuck fast too!

So now here he is, bottle up the arse and finger in the bottle. What an idiot!

Of course the staff remained professional throughout. After picking themselves back off the floor and getting a mop to clear the collective piss from excessive laughter, they agreed to help. First they needed to check out his story. After all, they would have looked pretty stupid had they turned up at hospital and it was all sick Smith's idea of a joke. Sure enough, after a swift bend by Smith, the neck was spotted and the laughter started again.

"Please help me," says Smith, "Don't tell anyone. This is so embarrassing." This was possibly the worst thing that Smith could have said. He might as well of told the officers to write what had happened on the wing notice board, to put it in the prison magazine, to call the national papers, such is the mentality of prison officers.

"Sure" said Jones. "We'd better call an ambulance."

During the commotion, interest had been generated among the other cons on the wing. Buzzers started sounding. People wanted to know what had disturbed their slumber.

"Please keep this quiet?" says Smith. "I really don't want this to come out".

"I should think that's exactly what you do want right now!" says Jonesy with another wicked smile breaking on his contorted face.

The S.O. retreated to call the ambulance and as he did so, Jones did his best to silence the others and comfort Smith.

As you will discover Officers can have a warped sense of humour and Jones had already come up with plans to make Smith regret his actions. He wanted to do something that would hopefully discourage any repetitions of this sick behaviour.

The five wings of this prison were laid out on one long corridor. They stuck out the back at right angles rather like floating pontoons off a jetty, or how a row of terraced houses would have their brick out houses attached at the back. This meant that each wing had lots of windows facing one another and all had a pretty clear view of the road that ran along the back to service them all.

The ambulance arrived and was told to go to the wing next door to Smiths. Not by mistake either.

In the meantime, Jonesy and the S.O. had their hands full trying to extricate Smith from his cell and ultimately his wing. The old boy was never that quick, but with 9 or 10 inches of glass and a finger up his arse his progress was painfully snail like. All the way down the stairs, (unfortunately for Smith he lived on the third floor), he kept going on about one thing. Surprisingly it wasn't the excruciating pain coming from his over stretched ring piece. No. He was adamant that no one sees him or knows what has happened.

"Don't worry!" says Jonesy slyly. "You're safe with us".
As the slow progress continued down the stairs, Smithy said,
"Please cover me. Have you got a blanket?"
A blanket was found and Smith adopted a cunning disguise. More slow progress. The pain was really kicking in now and Smith was finding it hard to walk, but eventually they reached the gate to the back of the wing.
Slowly opening the gate Jones poked out a mischievous face to make sure that the ambulance was parked far enough away.
"Come on Smithy you're nearly there"
As he stepped foot out of the gate, Jonesy grabbed the blanket and whizzed it off and round his head like a depraved Matador. As he did he started shouting wildly.
"Look at this everybody. Look out of the windows. Look! Look!" Jonesy was in his element, and there was no stopping him now. His commotion had the desired effect as faces started appearing at windows and heads were poked out to get a better look. They were met with the site of Smith looking like a horrified and embarrassed man with a finger up his arse. In fact it was far worse than that. There was of course a bottle involved but from the acute angled view afforded by the other con's vantage point, they couldn't see the neck.
At this point a very strange metamorphosis took place. Smith changed from a bumbling old git slowed by the pain of his predicament, to a 100-meter athlete not dissimilar to Linford Christie apart from the obvious displacement of his food receptacle! He accelerated down the track, sorry I mean road, towards the waiting ambulance and by the time he launched himself into the back, he was but a blur. All this, still completely naked

and with his finger firmly stuck where the sun doesn't shine! Dumbstruck with laughter the officers finally caught him up and escorted him to hospital. The cheers and shouts of the other cons lucky enough to witness the bizarre race echoed around the grounds for quite some time.

It didn't end there. Needless to say, Smith's predicament caused as much of a stir in the hospital as it did the prison. It's said that every member of the NHS staff on duty that night were called in to the examination room. Not to give their valued and professional opinions but to witness something they could tell their Grand kids in years to come. Everyone from the top surgeon to the toilet cleaner came in to have a good look, much to Smith's annoyance.
I'll spare you the gory details of how the muscle relaxing injection was administered and the bottom finally fell out of Smith's world. Or was it the world falling.........

The story did make one of the National papers. I'll leave you to guess which one? But worse still was the piss taking from both staff and con's that poor old Smith was made to endure. Who, for the next few months at least, was known as Saucy.

<u>SuperGran</u>

Every prison has a visits hall. This is where prisoners can see members of their family or friends for up to a couple of hours at a time. Usually a prisoner can get a few visits a month if their people are willing to come up to see them that often. It is a great way for prisoners to keep in touch with the outside world, to strengthen family ties and remind them of what they are missing.

Unfortunately, it is also the gateway to smuggle drugs into the prison. Not content with just seeing their family and friends for a chat, a small percentage pressure and threaten them into bringing in drugs. The signs are there for all to see. If caught, they risk anything up to 10 years in prison for supplying a prisoner, but still they do it. Many reasons are given for this behaviour. The con will tell his family he is being threatened on the wing and fears for his life. This really means, he has got a drug habit and is in debt to the dealers so needs some gear brought in to help pay off his debt. He will say he is being bullied and has to bring the gear in for someone else. This really means, he has set up a nice little business selling drugs on the wing and needs his family to produce a plentiful supply. Whatever the reason, it is wrong. It is the scourge of the prison system and causes more problems inside than anything else.

 Bearing all this in mind, consider the story you are about to read and try to understand the mentality the staff have to deal with on a day to day basis.

 Mrs. Smith was well into her sixties. She was a kindly looking old lady that kept herself in good nick. She always made the effort to look good, but the years had not been kind and despite the effort she made, her age showed. About 5' 2" she looked much shorter because of her curved back. Her skin was wrinkled and this was mirrored in her ironing which was not her best skill. Her expensive, though crumpled and musty clothes, gave her the look of a glamorous bag lady, the kind you might find sleeping in the doorway of Harrods or Selfridges.

There was not much to distinguish her from any other visitor. In fact she had been here before on a number of occasions and was well known by the staff. There was no reason to suspect her of doing anything wrong.

Visits was in full swing when Mrs. Smith arrived. She had come to see her son, Smith.

The room used for visits was large and roomy and was always busy, especially on weekends. There were a number of entrances to the room. One led to the search area, where any prisoners coming in or going out could be stopped and searched. Everyone entering would be subject to a rub down search. This involves an officer patting down the prisoner over the top of his clothes. Any prisoner leaving the visits would be strip-searched. This time the prisoner had to remove his clothing, top half first, then the bottom half. The officer would visually check the prisoner while looking through the articles of removed clothing. This is one of the worst parts of an officer's duties. It is always a potential flash point as the prisoners are never happy to remove their clothes in front of staff. I can see their point. I would hate to have to do this and would feel embarrassed if not degraded. Most of the staff would try to be as diplomatic as possible but there was always the odd one or two that would make a scene and make the job harder for the others.

Any visitors entering the hall are also subject to a rub down search. This is just as important as searching the prisoners, as there is a big chance that drugs may be entering along with the visitor. For years they would bring the drugs in hidden in their clothes. Then the prisons started using drug dogs to combat the heavy trafficking. Drug carrying techniques were changed to get round this inconvenience and quite extreme they are too. The majority of it comes in "Plugged" This is a prison term for hiding the drug in a body orifice. The women have an unfair advantage when it comes to plugging, making full use of their front and back botties, where as men can only use the one hole. Bringing drugs into the hall in this way has a number of advantages.

1) The hole of choice has its own airtight seal so that the dog can detect no drug aroma, although the remnants or residue can also be detected on hands or clothing. With some more unsavoury characters, there is also a nasty niff from that hole, that helps mask the smell of the drug, but enough said about that, the better.
2) The drugs can be comfortably transported until the time is right to make the pass.
3) The front orifice is usually larger than the back so can store multiple drops. These can be passed to multiple recipients, thus achieving multiple happiness amongst the cons involved.

The offending visitor will generally go to the toilet and remove the hidden item, then try bringing it back into the hall to make the pass. The con will take the item and do his best to stick it where the sun don't shine before the always observant officers jump all over him to try to retrieve whatever it is that has been passed. It happens day in, day out. Sometimes staff catch them, sometimes they don't. One thing is for sure. The introduction of the drug dog has made it much easier for staff to detect the carriers, before they enter.

 As Mrs Smith entered the search area she was greeted with the usual niceties that the staff in that area were used to dispensing. There was talk of the weather, the cat wasn't well and Mrs. Smith's bunions had been playing up terribly over the last couple of weeks. She was just a lovely, cuddly little old lady. The drug dog was indicating otherwise. Modern dogs are trained to casually walk along a line of people and nonchalantly sit down when it gets a whiff of any drugs. Old style dogs were a bit different to that. As soon as they smelt drugs, it was game on. They knew they would be rewarded and were taught to show excitement. This particular dog was bloody good at its job. A bit too good sometimes. On this occasion it didn't take an expert to realise that the dog had found something as all you could see was its tail wagging from under Mrs Smith's skirt. In fact, if the officer didn't have such a tight grip on the over enthusiastic hound, he may well have gone to ground and Mrs. Smith would need him surgically removed. She showed no emotion, but simply blamed it on the fact that she owned a few cats and the dog could obviously smell them.
 Now, when such a strong indication is noted, the staff are required to carry out a strip search. Again this is a very dodgy part of the job, and requires a lot of tact and diplomacy. Obviously the two male officers on duty that

day could not carry out the search and would have to call for two females. While this was being done, the lads tried their best to explain to Mrs Smith that she really should come clean and own up to what she had on her. All the time they were doing this, they feared for their jobs for two reasons.

1) Because they really didn't think that Mrs. Smith, at her age, would be daft enough to bring drugs in.
2) Because they were scared they would lose the drug dog, such was its keenness to disappear like a rat up a pipe.

"Please Mrs. Smith, close your legs, the dog will need to be bathed later and I was supposed to be going out for a drink with the boys." Said Browny in desperation.
"It must be my cat's dear. He obviously partial to an old pussy," she kept saying as nothing out of the ordinary was happening. "Isn't his nose cold, what an enthusiastic boy. Reminds me of my old Cedric, god rest his soul."
"Mrs Smith do you have any drugs hidden about your person."
"No dear. I'm too old for all that messing about. I just want to see my son. He's a lovely boy you know. Never been any trouble. Do you know him? Lovely boy."
 As the questioning from the officers continued Mrs. Smith became more obscure with her answers.
"Mrs. Smith, the dog is indicating that you may have drugs on you. Is that correct Mrs. Smith." Said Jonesy.
"I haven't been down the Legion for months. Got fed up with the bingo."
"Mrs. Smith, I fail to see what that has do with this situation. Do you have any drugs?"

"I've got three cats, two Budgies and a Tortoise. Never owned a dog"

"Not a dog Mrs. Smith. Do you have any drugs?"

At this point reinforcements arrived in the form of the two lady officers called for earlier.

They took Mrs Smith into a side-room and continued questioning her. She continued with her bizarre answers. It was time to call the police.

"Mrs. Smith we have called the police because we believe that you may be carrying drugs about your person. If you do not agree to a strip search by us, you will be taken away to have one carried out at the police station." Said Sharon, who was one of the ladies called to help out. " I can assure you Mrs. Smith that they will be a lot rougher than us. We are very sympathetic to this sort of thing and if you do have anything I will do everything I can to help you," she reassured.

The severity of the situation started to dawn on Mrs. Smith and she finally looked as if she was listening.

"Do you have any drugs on you Mrs. Smith?" Sharon repeated.

"Of course I have" Mrs. Smith admitted for the first time. "My son told me that he was going to be stabbed if I didn't bring them up for him. He said that people were going to get him as he owed them lots of money. He said I was the only one who could help him and that I should bring some drugs for him." It all came flooding out like a dam bursting after a particularly heavy downpour.

"At last we are getting somewhere. Now Mrs. Smith, just pop behind that screen and you can remove whatever it is you have without us even needing to touch you."

Off she went. It was a bit hard for her to walk as the dog was now half way in and was digging for his reward.

"Get that pissing dog out of here Browny, he's putting her off"

Officer Brown gave a sharp yank on the lead and the Retriever was retrieved.

It was time for action. Before long and after various slurping noises from behind the screen, Mrs. Smith handed over a small slimy package.

Outside of prison, drug prices can vary from region to region. Inside the prison they go up x10. Because of demand, the required quantities are just not available. So everything costs ten times as much. Cannabis was always the most sought after but after the introduction of random urine testing the most popular drug quickly became Heroin. The reason for this is that Cannabis stays in the system for up to a month whereas Heroin is undetectable after 48 hours. Fed up with being caught by the tester and thus receiving extra days on the sentence, prisoners in their droves turned to Heroin for their kicks but found they quickly became addicted. This as you may realise caused more problems than it solved. Instead of prisons full of laid back potheads, we have prisons full of uptight smack heads that would stab anyone just to get their next fix.

You can imagine the surprise when Mrs. Smith produced a fairly substantial lump of Cannabis with a prison value of 2 or 3 hundred pounds.

"Thank you Mrs. Smith. This has saved us a lot of problems. You can get dressed now and we will wait for the police. We will tell them how co-operative you have been."

"That's not it." Said Mrs. Smith from behind the screen as the squelching continued.

"Are you saying you have something else Mrs. Smith," said Sharon in amazement.

She was saying that, and before long another slimy package was passed around the screen into the gloved hand of Sharon's friend Tracey.

This one was smaller than the first, but was more sinister as it was instantly recognisable as Heroin. Outside this may have been worth a couple of hundred pounds but inside it was worth about £2000.

"Good grief," said Sharon and Tracy together as they examined the smelly parcel. "She's a walking bloody chemist"

"That's not it," said the voice form behind the screen. Sharon popped her head round to check there wasn't a magician's hat or something lying about.

"I've got more", said Mrs. Smith in a nervous and croaky voice. Another even slimier parcel was handed round the screen into waiting hands of the staff. Again smaller but this was not instantly recognisable. The package was bumpy and white and seemed to be full of small stones. She didn't realise it at the time but Mrs. Smith was the first person to bring Crack Cocaine into the prison. This was something none of the assembled staff had ever seen before. Mind you Mrs. Smith was something no one in the prison service had seen before. Just when they thought there could be no more,

"That's not it. There's more"

"You're taking the piss now," blurted Tracy, as she stood with her mouth open as wide as her disbelieving eyes. "Where's the bloody camera? We being filmed for telly or something?"

Unfortunately they weren't. What they were witnessing was all true. A poor old lady had been duped into bringing in drugs by her son. He didn't tell her what to bring, he just said drugs. He didn't stipulate how much. She just went out and bought whatever she could with her savings. Quite how Smith would have coped with the amount of gear his mum had bought up was beyond me. He wouldn't have dreamed in a million years she would have come in with so much. The best he could have hoped for was a quarter ounce of Cannabis of a gram of Heroin.

The next item on Mrs. Smith's conveyor belt was a package containing Acid Tabs. These were a hallucinogenic substance and were very rare in prisons. Acid is mainly taken amongst groups of friends. It is not the best drug to take on your own as the taker often experienced a "bad trip" which can be a very frightening experience. But Mrs. Smith didn't give a shit about that. She was on a roll. Her vagina packed, drug cocktail was coming along nicely. There wasn't many more drugs she could have got. But then,

"This is the last bit." Still there was more. Her fanny was like Felix the Cat's Bag. It was an Aladdin's cave of illegal pharmaceuticals. How could she have more? Out came a small package of Sulphate commonly known as Speed.

Well she really had excelled herself. She had single handily and unwittingly supplied enough gear to suit every craving in the prison for the next couple of months.

The police took her and her sack full of swag to the police station forthwith.

It was a good few months later when Jonesy was asked to do an escort to the local Crown Court. It was unusual, as this Prison didn't often do local Crown Court runs as most of the clientele were from out of the area. He picked up the prisoner from his wing and took him to reception. This is the place where all the cons either enter or leave the prison. As they got chatting, Jonesy began to realise that this may be the son of Mrs. Smith who should have received the skip full of drugs that his blackmailed mum tried to bring in all that time ago. Of course, there was going to be a court case with Mrs. Smith as the defendant. Smith must be going down to give evidence. The poor old lady could be looking at a few years inside. Obviously Smith would be going down to explain what had happened. He would tell the judge and jury that he had put her up to it. He would explain how he got into debt in prison to the drug dealers, and he had been threatened and feared for his life. It was all his idea. His poor unsuspecting mother was just the poor sod who had been dragged in to it all by her unscrupulous son. Everything will be explained and she will be okay.

 As the staff walked their man up into the witness box, Jonesy spotted Mrs. Smith standing there in tears. She was now the defendant in her own court case. It was no longer her son she had to watch going through the same old motions. It was she that was now in deep trouble. Smith would tell the truth and get her out of this mess. Jonesy was sure of it!

"Mr Smith. I want you to tell the court in your own words, what happened on the day your mother visited," the judge boomed after Smith had been sworn in.

"Well your honour. It's like this. I told the stupid cow not to do it. She's always doing it. She tries to get me in trouble all the time. She asked me if I needed any drugs and I said no! I haven't touched any gear for years. That silly bitch is the one on the gear." He pointed to the little

old lady standing there crying in the dock, his own
mother and laughed as the judge said,
"Take her down."

Up On The Roof

"I'm sure I just saw a head pop over the edge of that roof" thought Jonesy to himself.

He was manning the route to work on a dank and dismal morning. When the cons were released from the wings to attend their places in the workshops, it is always necessary for a handful of officers to take up key positions along the route from the wings to the shops. Prisoners have a tendency to wander off or dawdle, especially Y.P's. These "Young Prisoners" are a breed apart from any other type of con. Having never worked with them, I cannot talk from experience, but you can imagine what it's like. You only have to walk around any street in any British town and you'll find a group of potential Y.P's. They will be in a huddle, usually swearing, spitting, smoking and now a more recent and far more sinister development, texting and happy slapping. As you approach, no matter how much you attempt to remain un-noticed, they will turn their short attention spans on you, hurling as much abuse as they can, from what limited vocabulary they have. After this they will knock over some old grannies, smash up some antique phone boxes, sniff some glue, smoke some dope, do a bit of graffiti, and all this before they have reached school in the morning. Put three or four hundred of these little buggers into a prison environment and you've got a recipe for disaster. These little shits will do nothing that is required of them without at least an argument but more often a fight. They will do all the things they are not supposed to do just for devilment and anything they can to upset the normal daily routine.

Jonesy was standing in the rain watching the usual idiotic antics of the Y.P's as they made their way to work. There was slightly more of a commotion than normal but nothing too much out of the ordinary. Just then, something caught Jonesy's eye. He wasn't known for his observational abilities, but he could not miss the obvious head peaking out over the edge of the boiler house roof. Now, he had a couple of options. He could call up on the radio straight away, which would probably attract the attentions of dozens of bored adolescents. Or he could have done what he did, and bide his time until they were all safely locked in their respective shops, then investigate further.

He told the other officers what he had seen and they all made their way stealthily over to the boiler house. Finding a convenient route, Jonesy climbed up and took a sneaky peek onto the roof and there in the far corner was Smith. He was lying on his stomach looking over the edge so didn't notice Officer Jones watching him. Jonesy scrambled back down, told the others what he'd seen and a plan was hatched for Smith's removal.

In the good old days, things were a lot easier to deal with. Health and safety rules and reg's have made easy jobs very hard. Specialist teams must be used these days for rooftop removals but back when this incident occurred there was no need for such unnecessary intervention. A few of the officers climbed onto the roof and made contact with Smithy. They were hoping that a show of strength may persuade him to give up his silly game. But no, he was having none of it. He backed off to the corner and started with the usual tirade of abuse that you would expect from a boy of his age. Would have probably thrown in a bit of texting too if he had a mobile to hand.

All the usual lengthy negotiations that take place at this stage failed.
"Smith are you coming down?"
"No, Fuck Off!"
"Right get him!!"
So they got him. At this point when totally outnumbered with the odds stacked against him any normal con would have given up but they were not dealing with normal, they were dealing with a Y.P. Smith fought like a Tiger. No one knew why, not even Smith, but the fight was on. It only took a matter of seconds to subdue him. Smith was not a big lad and because of the drizzle, the officers were in no mood to mess about. The normal routine would normally kick in at this point, that covers all prisoner removals. The con, now in locks, (wrist locks) would be walked, or carried if he refused to walk, to the Seg where he would be located in a strip cell if he was non compliant. But this was no ordinary removal. Smith and the accompanying officers were 20 feet up on the boiler house roof, with no way down. This was going to take some thought.

By this time further staff had arrived accompanied by a P.O. ready to take charge of the developing situation. This P.O. was a very well respected member of staff and was well known for his no-nonsense approach. He didn't suffer fools easily. For this the staff loved him and the con's hated him with a passion. He climbed onto the roof to access the situation and it took just a matter of minutes to weigh up the multitude of options available to him, but the one he chose surprised even the hardest of his assembled colleagues. He instructed the staff that had hold of the squelching, gibbering wreck that loosely resembled Smith, to walk over to the edge of the roof, near to where a heap of coal was stacked. Once near the edge, he instructed other officers to stand near the coal, (on ground level) and ready themselves. For what, they wasn't yet sure. He then ordered the staff on the roof to release Smith straight away. They were shocked at this request but did what they were told.

"Catch" shouted the P.O. to the staff on the ground as he grabbed a startled Smithy and hurled him with great force off the edge of the roof.

This was better than the bird man of Alcatraz. For a few seconds Smithy actually flew. But not for long, no sooner had he hit the wet coals below, he was covered in a swarm of cold wet officers, willing to take him to his new cell in the block.

Mum Sent a Letter!

For day's now, Smith had been moaning at the officer door he had not received the money his mum sent in. Each prisoner is allowed to have money. This comes from the wages that they earn or from cash sent in by family or friends. They don't actually hold the cash. It's put into an account. They are issued with a canteen sheet on which they can fill out a sort of shopping list for the things they want to purchase each week. There are limits to the amount they can spend and there is also a limited list of the things they can buy. Most con's though are easily pleased with the most basic of commodities, Tobacco and phone units.

The usual routine for getting money in was quite easy to follow. The sender just has to include their name and address as well as the name and number of the intended payee. It was quite simple. But we are not dealing with everyday people here. If the money arrived with no senders details (as it often did) it would be booked into the withheld cash book until such time the sender was contacted to confirm their details.

All that is usually needed is a brief letter confirming who they are, their address and it was them that sent it. So, it was a bit unusual that Smith's money had not found its way into his account after a couple of weeks and his incessant moaning. A few more days of whining passed when officer Jones decided enough was enough and he would phone the post room. Staff didn't like doing this for two very different reasons.

1) Once they had made that call it suddenly became their responsibility to find and retrieve the missing payment. Well not officially it wasn't but to the

penniless con, you were now his point of contact. His saviour who would reunite him with his missing loot. He would hound you, follow you and moan like a bitch until the only way you could shut him up was to find that money!

2) There was a very strange lady working in the post room who was so utterly useless you sometimes wondered if she was taking the piss!? Dealing with anything with that lady was like pulling teeth but she was your only choice when finding missing mail.

Jonesy phoned.

"Hello post room" said the dizzy sounding woman in the post room.
Jonesy explained the circumstances as clearly and as simply as he could. Strange lady said there was £20 in the withheld book for Smith but she was waiting for a letter to confirm who it came from. Hoping for an unusually easy result, Jonesy relayed this back to Smith who said,
"My mum sent a letter!"
"Well there's no letter here for Smith" strange lady whined and put the phone down.
"Will you try again for me tomorrow boss?"
Jonesy was caught. Snared in the money chasing trap!

"Remind me tomorrow" he said in true "I'll forget by then" prison officer style. But remind him he did, every hour. Each call that was made got the same response, day after day for another week. Smith kept saying,

"My mum sent a letter!" Not the sharpest knife in the drawer was Smithy, not much of a conversationalist.

About a week after the initial call Jonesy was at the end of his tether. He called strange lady and asked her to take her daily look. At this point she revealed that there had indeed been a letter there for a few weeks. Well it was more of a note really. You can see why there may have been some confusion. The note read,

Dear Governor,

I sent my son £20.

From Mary.

With parents like that you can understand why Smith was in prison. There was no name other than Mary, no prison number, nothing to identify either the sender or the person it was for.

Jonesy asked Smith what's his mum's first name?

"Mary. Why?"

Weeks of moaning and stress for this......

"C" Wing Stabbing

"Urgent Message" is something you really don't want to hear over the radio! The word message, on its own, is bad enough. It is seldom used as it is primarily saved for when something important needs to be broadcast. When used, it's enough to grab the attention of anyone within earshot of a radio. But coupled with the "U" word, it means that there is a serious problem somewhere or someone is in imminent danger and all available staff must attend immediately.

The night Jonesy heard it for the first time was a night he would never forget. He had no idea quite how urgent that cry for help was until he arrived on scene. No idea of the impact it would have on his life for years to come. It all went down like this.

Officer Jones was escorting two trusted prisoners back along the central corridor after taking the food trolley back to the kitchen. Over the radio came the shout, "Urgent message! All available staff report to "C" Wing immediately."
He instantly took the decision that he had to go. He trusted the two lads to return to their wing unaccompanied. Usually you cannot attend an alarm bell if you are already in charge of prisoners but as it was an urgent call, he felt it a necessary risk.

Jonesy ran straight to "C" Wing where the gate was already open and was directed to the 2's landing (2nd floor) by the officer guarding the gate. As he ran up the stairs he could hear shouting. There was an unusually large amount of prisoners hanging around all the way up the steps. On arrival at the 2's, there was water all over the floor, a lot more loitering prisoners and an awful moaning coming from somewhere. His instincts were already telling him there was something seriously wrong. An officer was standing outside cell 208, the first on the left along the middle spur. The landing was laid out in a T shape with the long spur in the middle. Seven cells to the left, seven to the right and fourteen down the middle. As he entered the cell he found an officer already present. The look of fear on his face was burned into Jonesy's memory there and then. He was sitting astride a writhing prisoner on the bed and was covered in blood. The whole cell was covered in blood. We're talking floor, walls and even the ceiling were covered in spatters of thick red blood. As Jonesy tried to take in the sight and subconsciously start to work out what had happened and what he should do, he was joined in the cell by one other male and two female officers. It was quiet in there except for the moaning and gargling from the prisoner who had obviously sustained a very serious stab wound. Jonesy noticed the floor was very sticky, and put that down to the amount of blood lying around but soon realized it was sugared water, commonly known within the prison system as "Napalm." It is often used in violent attacks to seriously disfigure. The sugar is dissolved in boiling water then thrown over the victims face. Normal water would badly scald the skin but because of the molten sugar the concoction sticks to the skin and continues to burn deeper so the flesh can actually peel away.

The silence was broken.

"How deep is the wound?" Jonesy asked Officer Brown

who was still on the bed with his hands over the prisoner's neck.

"It's really bad" Brown said with panic in his voice.

"How bad? Let me have a look." Jonesy said. He was a well weathered Officer with a lot of experience of assaults and attacks, with a good solid First Aid background. As Brown eased the blood soaked towel he had grabbed to use as a dressing, to one side, a powerful spurt of blood gushed from the gaping hole in the prisoner's neck. It splashed up the wall and dripped from the corner of the ceiling like some hellish stalactite.

"Shit that's bad!" said Jonesy, "Cover it up!"

The blood flow was massive. The prisoner's clothing and bedding were soaked red as were the clothes of the staff. S.O. White was now on the bed and was trying to hold the prisoner still. He was losing consciousness but was thrashing around violently. Although he had not uttered a word since the arrival of the staff or opened his eyes, it was as if he knew he had been the victim of an awful attack and was still fighting for his life. White was having a hard time holding down his legs. The prisoner was a good 6' 6", weighing around 18 stone and was incredibly strong even in this vulnerable condition.

The two girls present were Deb and Tracy. Both had been in the service for a fair few years but had never had to deal with an attack as serious as this. Deb was holding the prisoners hand and talking to him trying to keep him awake, while Tracy was very busy opening more and more dressings to use to stem the flow of blood.

Jonesy had to act fast! He had arrived on a situation where staff were in control but were not pulling together as a team, the work was fragmented and unorganised.

"You've got to stop that bleeding mate" he calmly said to Browny. "But you've got to stop pressing so hard on his neck. You're compressing his windpipe and stopping him breathing."

No one was sure if the weapon had punctured the windpipe as everything was such a mess but his breathing was becoming more laboured. It could have been down to the pressure being applied or the throat was filling up with blood. Either way he was chocking badly.

"If you don't want to do it, I will. But you're gonna have to poke your fingers down into the wound to try to stop the blood flowing directly from the vein." Jonesy was up for it but wanted to give Browny the chance to continue his excellent work.

A look of horror and panic appeared on Browny's face but he hurriedly agreed to do it. The prisoner was really thrashing around now which didn't help this next manoeuvre. Slowly Browny eased his hand under the pile of blood soaked dressings and slid two fingers into the gaping hole. The blood poured out from under the dressing. Jonesy joined the trio on the bed to try to secure the prisoners arms. Browny's fingers squished in further but could find no end to the hole. Blood continuously squirted in all directions.

"I can't do it! I can't slow it down!" shouted Browny. "Feel around! Move your fingers until the hole is sealed!!" and after a minute or so of this blind fumbling the flow started to ease but only slightly. Time was of the essence.

More officers were arriving to the scene all the time. Inside the cell, it was like time had stood still. Unbeknown to the 5 officer's inside the cell there was bedlam outside on the landing. It was clear there had been a very serious assault. The arriving staff had a number of things to consider. There was a load of prisoners out on the landing. It was the middle of association time where all prisoners on the wing are unlocked to socialise, play pool, table tennis etc. but it seemed all of them were up there on the landing enjoying the spectacle. They were shouting and jostling and seemed very excited about what they had seen. The first thing for staff was to get these prisoners locked away and it didn't matter where they were secured. Usually you would only lock a prisoner in his own cell but the landing needed to be cleared immediately. Officers pushed, persuaded and cajoled all the cons into any cell they were near.

Some cells now contained as many as five prisoners, which could cause serious repercussions later but there was more important work to do now.

Another thing to consider was preservation of evidence. Whatever it was that caused that awful wound was a very serious weapon and needed to be found. Staff were tasked with searching the landing's, recesses, showers and all areas outside the wing, as stuff was regularly thrown from the windows. It was very dark outside so searching the grounds was not easy. It was lashing down with rain too further hampering the search and washing away any potential evidence.

Some officers took charge of trying to piece together the evening's events to try to work out what may have happened, who would have carried out such a vicious attack and what the hell was the motive.

Inside the cell, things were getting desperate. The

prisoner was fighting and thrashing around unnaturally considering his condition. S.O. White and Jonesy were being knocked to the floor and smashed off the walls as they tried to restrain the dying mans arms and legs. He kept grabbing at his own neck and pulling away the dressings stemming the blood flow. He was obviously in serious pain but worse he seemed to be gasping for breath. Each time he pulled at Browny's hands, thick spurts of blood spattered over the bed, walls, officers and floor. The Officers white uniform shirts were now unrecognisable as they were sodden with bright red blood.

"He's gonna die!" shouted Browny.

"Just stay calm. We're doing all we can. We gotta stay controlled to stand any chance of saving him!" assured Jonesy.

As soon as they sent out the "Urgent Message" call over the radio, the staff in the control room contacted the emergency services and an ambulance was dispatched immediately. It wasn't long before sirens could be heard approaching the prison.

The five officers battling to save the life of the man in their care heard nothing but his desperate cries and moans as he drifted further away.

With all the other prisoners secured behind cell doors, more officers assembled at the door of 208. One of them was taking notes and keeping an accurate record on what was going on inside and outside of the cell. Suddenly, an officer who had been searching outside the wing appeared on the landing. He was carrying what looked like a couple of wet woollen hats. It turned out to be four homemade Balaclavas or masks. They were indeed woollen type hats but they had eye and nose holes cut out of them. With this bit of vital information, the officer's now knew it was probably a well planned attack by at least four masked men. Also on the floor of the cell were a couple a plastic jugs. These were probably used at the start of the attack. They would have been filled with sugar water and thrown all over the prisoner as a distraction. Jonesy noticed deep burns appearing on the head, neck and hands of his patient. He suspected his face would be in an awfully similar state but with so much blood covering everything it was impossible to tell at this stage just how bad the burns were. These would have to be dealt with later if indeed the man survives!?

Two paramedics were escorted to the cell. Jonesy jumped up and did his best to describe everything that had happened. He explained the extent of the injuries and told them about the condition of the prisoner, his laboured breathing, his burns but most concerning the apparent bottomless hole in his neck. They quickly went to work checking the casualty and witnessed the same spurt of blood from around Browny's fingers when they checked the wound. They realised from the amount of blood everywhere, they had to move. NOW!

An S.O. had been asking around for volunteers to escort the prisoner to the hospital with the Paramedics. Most of them though were reluctant partly because of the amount of claret involved but mostly because of the likelihood this guy was not going to survive. The paperwork would be horrendous. Many of them had been on duty since 07.00 and this looked like it was going to be an all-nighter.

Jonesy stepped up to the plate.

"I'll go with him! I might as well. I'm already covered in blood and I can pass on all I know at the hospital."

The S.O. was reluctant to use Jonesy as he had been through a very stressful situation already but had very little choice. Soon as Jonesy had volunteered one of his mates, Ian, agreed to go with him.

A chair was brought up from the ambulance and with a great deal of effort and difficulty the dead weight of the thrashing prisoner was man handled onto it, then was strapped on to keep him still. Officers and Paramedics then had the difficult job of carrying the dead weight down two flights of stairs. Jonesy took over from Brown and took hold of the sodden rags pressed over the wound. Even strapped into the chair, the huge prisoner still caused problems as the guys tried to carry him down to the waiting ambulance. He was completely incoherent and had no idea what was going on around him. He had completely lost consciousness some time ago but was still thrashing and fighting for life.

As they got to the ground floor, Jonesy noticed for the first time since entering the wing, that a lot of prisoners had been contained within the communal association area downstairs. This was a large room containing pool tables and T.V's, where many of the prisoners would have been while the assault took place upstairs. The wall on this end was constructed with large observation windows for staff to keep an eye on what was happening inside. Suddenly it became a macabre freak show. As soon as the prisoners locked inside the room saw the injured man appear in front of them, they started jeering and booing as if they knew him and hated him with a vengeance. As he was carried out of the wing and outside to the ambulance, there was venomous shouts of "Nonce" and "Bacon." Both commonly used words within the prison system to describe someone who was serving sentences for crimes such as Rape, Sexual Assault or Paedophilia. Could this be the reason why he was stabbed? Was he a sex offender? Jonesy had no idea. He didn't know him from Adam. He seldom worked on "C" wing and didn't know many of the prisoners on there. Right at that time, Jonesy couldn't care less who he was; he just had to do what he could to save the man's life. It was his job! It was also the natural reaction of any human being to try to save another. He ignored the abuse from the windows. The prisoners were clearly pissed off that this guy was being helped. The paramedics and two officers bundled the stabbed man into the back of the vehicle and secured him on a trolley. Jonesy and Ian continued to hold him down. A drip was opened and one of the medic's tried to locate a vein to attach it to. It was virtually impossible as all his veins and arteries were collapsing due to huge blood loss. There was almost no fluid left inside the tubes to keep them flowing. Finally a needle was pushed into a larger vein in his ankle and the drip was connected.

A Principal Officer arrived with a bag containing all the usual escort equipment, paperwork, phone, cuffs, cuff keys, inserts (to be used in conjunction with the cuffs on smaller or thinner wrists) and a closeting chain (to be applied if the prisoner needs to use the toilet to allow him distance from the officer, made up of two halves of a conventional cuff with a length of chain between these. One end attached to the officer, the other to the prisoner). This was immediately applied to the prisoner in the ambulance and to Ian's wrist. It seemed incredibly unlikely that the stabee would try to run away at this stage but it was prison protocol that every prisoner being escorted from the front gate must be secure. There was no time for arguments. The chain allowed valuable space for the medics to work and saved Ian from being thrown around by the thrasher. The driver jumped in the front, fired up the engine and was escorted quickly to the front gate. The officer's key's and radios were quickly taken from them, blue lights flashed, sirens howled and the ambulance shot up the drive at break neck speed.

In the back of the van everyone was busy. Jonesy and Ian were still attempting to keep the prisoner still. Even after all this time he was still writhing around like a Boa Constrictor squeezing down on its prey. Back in the cell, there were five of them holding him still, now with only two, it was virtually impossible. Jonesy was still trying to stem the flow of blood even though the wound had been professionally dressed and packed by the medics. They hurtled through the near-by town and out into the countryside on route to the nearest A&E department. Suddenly everyone in the back flew forward as the driver slammed his breaks on and pulled into a lay by. There, waiting in that parking area was another Paramedic. Jonesy assumed it was someone more senior or experienced in this type of emergency. As soon as he was in the back, the vehicle shot off to cover the further four miles to the A&E. The new guy went to work straight away and grabbed more bags of Saline. Jonesy had never seen this done before. He attached the bag of fluid to the line in the prisoner's leg and squeezed the bag hard. The Saline disappeared into the leg practically within seconds. He pulled the empty bag off the line and repeated the process another four or five times! Jonesy didn't realise you could get fluid into a body that quick! The new Paramedic was seriously worried about the collapsing veins. The prisoner's internal organs were shutting down. He also suspected the weapon had been so long that it penetrated down through the left lung and possibly punctured some other organs. The lung had collapsed and the chest cavity was filling with blood. He was close to death.

A few minutes later the trolley and five rescuers flew into the A&E and was met by the waiting crash team. Picked up and dropped onto the bed, the prisoner was still thrashing around and omitting an awful deathly moan. It was more like convulsions now but Jonesy and Ian still had to hold him down. After what seemed like hours but was just a few minutes, everyone headed off to an operating theatre. There was no time for sterile gowns or gloves for the two prison officers. They were just dragged along with the trolley and continued their work to keep the prisoner still while various doctors took turns to look at the wound, prod it, poke it, stick various things down inside it, then stand and talk about what they should do with it. Jonesy was amazed how quiet and calm they all were. No one seemed to be doing anything to actually help the man. Then Jonesy noticed something else he had never seen before and hoped to never see again. There was neat saline trickling from the now open wound before him. After spending the last hour trying to stem the flow of blood from the injured man, Jonesy stood and witnessed the very last drop of blood leaving his body. Surely this was not possible? How was he still alive? There was only the clear salt solution circulating through his veins. Surely he was dead for sure?

Suddenly an older looking nurse stepped forward and shouted,

"For fuck's sake! If someone doesn't do something immediately, this man is going to die now!"

There was deathly silence. Then the doctors, surgeons and nurses jumped into action. Blood was rapidly pumped into various lines due to the need to get blood back into his system so quickly. The prisoner was injected with various drugs and attached to machines that took over his breathing for him. He was now finally still, completely unconscious and fully in the hands of the medical professionals.

Jonesy stepped forward and carefully removed the cuff from the prisoner's wrist that had kept them physically and spiritually linked during the trauma. Shell shocked and drained from what they had witnessed for the last hour, the two officers wandered into the corridor to rest but their ordeal was far from over.

Jonesy used the mobile phone to contact the prison and was put straight through to the Governor in charge.

"Is he dead?" asked the Governor.

"No. But I can't see him surviving if I'm honest," Said Jonesy, honestly.

"Are you two guys ok?" asked the Gov.

"Yeah top of the world," joked Jonesy, "Never better! Could do with a change of clothes, it looks like we've been working in an abattoir."

"I've got staff on their way to relieve you and stay with the prisoner overnight, if he survives. You two need to come straight back here, the police want to speak to you both."

No sooner had Jonesy hung up the call then their relief arrived. They quickly showed them to where the prisoner was being treated. Handed over cuffs, keys and paperwork etc and rushed out to the waiting taxi.

"Fuck me! You ain't getting in here like that!!" Shouted the driver when he saw the blood spattered officers.

"It's alright it ain't ours," said Jonesy, "We ain't gonna bleed anywhere and we'll be careful where we sit. Just get it cleaned up tomorrow and send the bill to the nick." Reluctantly he drove them back to the prison and dropped them at the gate. The place was swarming with Coppers! They were everywhere. Cars and vans all over the car park, uniform and plain clothes officers in the gate and all over the visits hall. All the members of staff on duty that evening were being interviewed. Anyone who had been directly involved had been relieved of their clothing and shoes as they were required for forensics. As soon as Jonesy entered the hall he was approached by two CID officers who sat him down and got him to go through the whole night's proceedings, right back from when he was in the corridor escorting the two trustees. It seemed to Jonesy like that was days ago, so much had happened since he started his shift at 07:30 but he did his best to remember all the details. Soon he was asked to remove his clothes, even his pants and socks as they may have carried just the slightest trace of DNA that could be used to identify the perpetrators. A thought crossed Jonesy's mind. He had been present at numerous assaults over the years, many of them serious, a lot of them involving staff but never before had he seen this unprecedented amount of police involvement. It seemed there was more interest in the capture of these prisoners, guys who would kill or maim each other for the promise of a bag of smack or if someone had committed the wrong crime. There was never this kind of response when a hard working, honest officer had been wrongfully assaulted.

Sitting in his new prisoners jog bottoms, shirt and slippers, Jonesy was getting the impression, due to the line of questioning he was being subjected to, that the prisoner who was attacked may have been so because an officer had told other prisoners what he was in for.

"How well did you know the prisoner?"

"Never seen him before in my life," Jonesy answered honestly. He had nothing to hide.

"But you work here every day, you must have seen him?"

"No. I generally work in a different area, another wing. I haven't done a shift on "C" wing for months."

"And how well do you know Officer Brown? How well did he get on with the prisoner?"

"I've known Browny since I started working here. And how the hell should I know how he gets on with the prisoners? I don't work on his wing!"

"So why were you here tonight? How come you were on the scene so quick?"

"As usual I answered the alarm bell, a call for help, as all available staff do. I got here quick as I'm a keen runner. I'm always quick!"

The questioning went on and all the time Jonesy was feeling like he had done something wrong. H e wasn't happy with some of the things the police were suggesting but knew he had to go through it. As it went on he had the growing feeling that they suspected his colleague Browny had in some way set the whole attack up.

It was gone 03:15 by the time Jonesy got home. Mrs. Jones was still wide awake. She had phoned in when her husband had not returned home after his shift that evening. She was used to him being late from time to time due to incidents in the prison but he would usually phone ahead so she didn't worry. Jonesy was mentally and physically shattered by now and after a very brief explanation of why he was wearing prisoners clothing and where he had been all night, he had a thorough shower and fell straight to sleep.

At 06:20 his alarm was bleeping loudly to signal the start of another working day. Usually after being out on an unplanned all night escort an officer would not be expected to turn up for the next day's duty. But today was different. Like the night before, the prison was swarming again with police officers. It seemed they had been there for some time and all available staff had been called in. Jonesy went in at 07:15 as usual as he knew his input would probably be required. He was there from the start of the incident to the very end and the info he held would be very important to the day's investigation. Amazingly, every single prisoner housed on "C" wing was being moved. One at a time, officers went to each cell door and explained to the occupant, they would have to get up and get dressed in disposable paper suits. Then they would leave the cell, taking no belongings and go with the officers downstairs where they would be interviewed by the police. They would then be taken to the reception area of the prison, commonly known as Reception, where they would join other "C" wing dwellers on one of the various vehicles that had turned up from umpteen prisons around the country and they would be transferred immediately.

Most were compliant fully with the instructions but as you can imagine there were many that were not happy with this early morning call. Some complained they had nothing to do with it and didn't want to be moved. Some wanted to take all their belongings with them. Some said the bloke who got stabbed was a nonce and they didn't give a fuck about him or the blokes that jumped him! But they had no choice, for a change the prison officers had the upper hand. Their numbers were strong and by opening prisoners one at a time, any resistance from within the cell was futile. They were going, like it or not! Within a couple of hours, the 67 prisoners left on the wing of 68 had gone. Now the huge police operation could commence. Every cell, room, store cupboard, server, TV room in fact every inch of the wing would eventually be searched. This was yet another thing Jonesy had never seen and never saw again.

It was only at this point after speaking to a few mates that Jonesy find out what had happened in those few hours he was asleep. The prisoner who was stabbed had been successfully operated on and had survived his attempted murder. Although a weapon was never found (well there were many weapons found during the search but none long enough to inflict this injury) it was suspected a broom handle sharpened to a point had been used. Lots of info had been gleaned from various prisoners about what they had seen or heard that night and more than a couple mentioned a long spike.

The spike had entered the prisoner's neck on the left side and severed the vessel that was taking oxygenated blood away from the brain. This meant he had a whole body's worth of fully oxygenated blood, pass through his brain before it left his new hole and at such high velocity it redecorated cell 208 so evenly. Very luckily with him being such a big guy, with an estimated 13 or 14 pints of oxygen rich blood passing through his twisted brain before the saline started to seep through, meant he survived with no brain damage. As time went by, everyone was amazed to hear he made a full recovery and was up and about in a matter of weeks.

Also from the information received on the morning of the big ship out, four names came up again and again. Some DNA was found that eventually connected the "C" wing 4 to the attempted murder of this known sex offender. Had Browny really told the cons about the prisoner's offence? Who knows? But it emerged that the attacked prisoners photo and story had appeared in a local paper only a week before the attack. This prison in fact held hundreds of local men so the attacker and victim were pretty well known. So maybe it was just a matter of time before the hate of his crimes caught up with him.

Six months later the "C" wing 4 were called to court to answer for their suspected attack. Jonesy and many other officers were called as witnesses. So many staff had to attend in fact, the prison had to be run on a limited regime that day. Of course the main witness was the man who was actually stabbed. He had been released from jail at this point and on the day of the trial he didn't even turn up! Apparently he had committed another sexual assault and would have been arrested for this latest crime if he turned up to give evidence against his attackers. How many chances do some people want!?

A year later, Jonesy, Browny, S.O. White and the two girls received Director Generals Commendations, the highest accolade awarded in the prison service, for their heroic actions that night. Martin Narey, who was DG at the time, handed them out during a prestige ceremony. The prison looked great in the glossy Prison Service magazine "Gatelodge" when the story and photos were printed.

The attackers were never brought to justice.
The prisoner who was stabbed was not seen again (at least at this prison). The officers involved got a nice certificate and a pen! Oh and suffered six months of stress and upset waiting for results of blood tests for HIV, Hep A B and C etc the list goes on. They had weeks of nightmares and sleepless nights due to a kind of Post Traumatic Stress Disorder. Even to this day, Officer Jones suffers recurring nightmares from the scenes he witnessed that night.

Printed in Great Britain
by Amazon.co.uk, Ltd.,
Marston Gate.